21-10-2017

To DEREK AND PAULINE

Best wishes and pleasant
reading during the pending
ashes tour of Australia

cheers

JOHN

THE POCKET HISTORY OF THE ASHES

Barry Nicholls

The
POCKET
HISTORY
of THE
ASHES

**All you need to know about
Cricket's greatest contest**

NH
NEW
HOLLAND

First published in 2017 by New Holland Publishers
London · Sydney · Auckland

The Chandlery, 50 Westminster Bridge Road, London SE1 7QY, United Kingdom
1/66 Gibbes Street, Chatswood, NSW 2067, Australia
5/39 Woodside Ave, Northcote, Auckland 0627, New Zealand

newhollandpublishers.com

A record of this book is held at the British Library and the National Library
of Australia.

ISBN 9781742572918

Group Managing Director: Fiona Schultz
Publisher: Alan Whiticker
Designer: Andrew Davies
Production Director: James Mills-Hicks
Printer: Hang Tai Printing Company Limited

10 9 8 7 6 5 4 3 2 1

Keep up with New Holland Publishers on Facebook
www.facebook.com/NewHollandPublishers

THIS BOOK IS DEDICATED TO

Charles Arthur Edward Mercer (1969–1999)
and Stephen Leslie Nicholls
who faced more than their share
of life's bouncers.

ACKNOWLEDGMENT

I would like to thank the always encouraging Alan Whiticker who asked me to undertake this project. The work of David Frith and Bill Frindall on earlier Ashes series in particular was invaluable as was the fact checking by the ever-vigilant statistician and general cricketing guru Lawrie Colliver, thanks mate. Chris Hamilton also reminded me of the importance of such a project. As always, my partner Ann and our beautiful, inquisitive children Jacy, Ambie, Harry and Ellie have been pillars of support. I hope you enjoy dipping into this small book as much as I enjoyed compiling it.

ABOUT THE AUTHOR

A former A grade district cricketer, Barry Nicholls has been writing about cricket for more than 20 years. Considered one of the premier thinkers and writers about the game, Nicholls has written seven books and contributed to *Inside Sport, Wisden Cricketer's Almanac Australia, Cricinfo, Cricket Lore, Inside Edge* and *Baggy Green*. Barry is also an award-winning broadcaster with the ABC where he has worked for 15 years. In addition to presenting a daily three hour drive show he also presented 110 Percent, a podcast about sports books for ABC Grandstand.

CONTENTS

HEADINGLEY, LEEDS 1980s

8

INTRODUCTION

We all have memories of our first or favourite Ashes contest. My introduction was the Adelaide Test of the 1970/71 series when Dennis Lillee took five wickets on debut, although the broad blade of England's opener Geoff Boycott was ever present. A favourite moment is harder to choose because there have been so many; perhaps Mark Waugh's debut ton in 1990/91, marking the arrival of one of Australia's most promising batting talents in years. His effortless stroke play was a delight for fans on an overcast otherwise slightly gloomy Adelaide day.

The phrase 'the Ashes' was born from a mock obituary in the British newspaper, *The Sporting Times* after defeat at the hands of the visiting Australians in 1882. Test cricket between the two nations began in 1877, resulting in an Australian win by 45 runs. However, five years later, the defeat of a full-strength England side including the great WG Grace at home by the colonials was another matter altogether.

The contest for the Ashes was given impetus by the England captain Ivo Bligh's wish to 'regain the Ashes' when he took a touring team to Australia later that year. England's win in the three official Tests resulted in a small urn being presented to Bligh by a group of women from Melbourne ... a group including Bligh's future wife Florence Murphy. Mystery remains over the contents of the burnt items contained in the Ashes urn, but the contest now had a symbol.

The idea of the Ashes becoming an entrenched symbol in Anglo-Australian cricket took some time to take hold, however. The Ashes held little traction for the most part of the 1800s. England captain Pelham 'Plum' Warner in 1904 revived the concept when he wrote a book about the series, *How We Recovered the Ashes*. Reporting

In Affectionate Remembrance

OF

ENGLISH CRICKET,

WHICH DIED AT THE OVAL

ON

29th AUGUST, 1882,

Deeply lamented by a large circle of sorrowing friends and acquaintances.

R. I. P.

N.B.—The body will be cremated and the ashes taken to Australia.

of subsequent series between England and Australia would more consistently refer to a 'fight' or 'battle' for the Ashes.

Over the years, there have been matches played between the two countries when the Ashes have not been at stake, most notably in 1979/80 after the reconciliation between Kerry Packer's World Series Cricket and the Australian Cricket Board, yet oddly when England hosted a triangular tournament with South Africa in 1912, the Ashes were up for grabs.

Ashes series trends show an early domination by England in the 1800s followed by an Australian revival at the turn of the century. England also suffered greatly after the enormous loss of lives during the First World War. Following some success in the late 1920s, England then had to cope with the overwhelming force of Australian batting sensation Don Bradman. It was Bradman who dominated for two decades (barring the 1932/33 Ashes) concluding when he led the 1948 'Invincibles' to a 4–0 victory.

One of the great aspects about Ashes cricket is not only the countless dramas but also the wonderful personalities, such as the flamboyant, former air serviceman Keith Miller and the equally charming Denis Compton who were as popular as any movie stars in the 1940s and 1950s. A decade later, the Ashes featured the tactical battles of Richie Benaud and Ted Dexter as each displayed their own match-winning abilities with bat and ball. The 1970s saw Ian Chappell and Tony Greig cement their places as Ashes legends as the encroaching player frustration grew, leading eventually to the advent of cricket's greatest crisis, the Kerry Packer inspired World Series Cricket.

Jumping years ahead, the excitement that the 2005 Ashes series generated revitalized what had been for so long a one-way contest in Australia's favour. England finally won back the Ashes in a series that showcased the talents of England all-rounder Andrew Flintoff and emerging star Kevin Pietersen. Scenes of the England team at Trafalgar Square in a double decker bus sparked memories of post war celebrations.

The Pocket History of the Ashes is designed to give some basic insight into the rich history of those who have been honoured to take part in one of the longest serving and greatest sporting rivalries of all time. It is not so much an analysis of the whys and wherefores but rather an essential account of the major events and the many record makers.

In a time when the future of Test cricket is in jeopardy because of the inundation of shorter forms of the game and cricket authorities continue to seek the commercial imperative above all else, the Ashes remains one of the few, if not the only, five Test match contest that continues to prove its value. May it long continue.

Barry Nicholls

CHAPTER 1

THE 1880s

ENGLAND, 1883

1882–83
IN AUSTRALIA

AUSTRALIA	V	ENGLAND
WL MURDOCH (1–4)		HON IFW BLIGH (1–4)
WON	DRAWN	WON
1 *		2

England, led by the Hon. Ivo Bligh, won what is considered to be
the first Ashes series. A fourth match was played against a United
Australian XI in which the home side succeeded but is recorded as
a standalone Test. Australia took the early lead in the series with a
nine wicket win and was helped by the big hitting of George Bonnor
scoring 85. Australia's 'Joey' Palmer, a medium-paced spinner took 10
for 126. England's Billy Bates became his country's first player to take
a Test hat-trick, finishing with 14 wickets for the match as well as a
half century. Bates' slow, roundarm bowling turning sharply from the
off, earned him £31 and a tall hat made of silver collected by his many
admirers. Nearly 23,000 attended the first day's play of the Third
Test at the Sydney Cricket Ground, which saw the visitors' Edmund
Tylecote score 66 and become the first keeper to score a half century.
Having successfully won back 'the Ashes' from WL Murdoch's 1882
touring side, England agreed to a fourth match in which Australia
held sway by four wickets.

* standalone Test, not part of the series

NEWSPAPER HEADLINE

Bligh Restores England's Honour!

THE SCOREBOARD

FIRST TEST: 30 December–2 January (Melbourne)
Australia won by 9 wickets
Australia 291 and 1–58
England 177 and 169

SECOND TEST: 19–22 January (Melbourne)
England won by an innings and 27 runs
England 294
Australia 114 and 153

THIRD TEST: 26–30 January (Sydney)
England won by 69 runs
England 247 and 123
Australia 218 and 83

FOURTH TEST: 17–21 February (Sydney) *
Australia won by 4 wickets
England 263 and 197
Australia 262 and 6 for 199

* standalone Test, not part of the series

FACEBOOK MOMENT

New South Wales batsman George Bonner became the first to be dismissed on 87 (Australia's 'devil number') after surviving being dropped eight times in the Fourth Test.

FOR THE RECORD

Most Runs:	AG Steel (ENG) 274
Most Wickets:	GE Palmer (AUS) 21
Highest Score:	AG Steel (ENG) 135 (Fourth Test)
Best Bowling:	W Bates (ENG) 7 for 28 (Second Test)
Most Catches:	GJ Bonnor (AUS), WL Murdoch (AUS),
	GB Studd (ENG) 4.
Highest Run	GJ Bonnor/G Giffen (AUS) 74
Partnership:	(Fourth Test, 4th wicket)
Centuries:	**England**
	AG Steel

TWITTER FACT

Billy Bates's hat-trick included the wickets of Percy McDonnell, George Giffen and George Bonnor.

DID YOU KNOW?

The captains decided to experiment by using a different pitch for each of the four innings of the fourth and final Test of the series. The Test is not recognised as an Ashes match but rather a standalone Test.

1884
IN ENGLAND

ENGLAND	V	AUSTRALIA
AN HORNBY (1), LORD HARRIS (2, 3)		WL MURDOCH (1–3)
WON	DRAWN	WON
1	2	0

Both Australia and England fielded strong sides with only three players debuting during the series. Manchester's first day of Test cricket was washed out while batsmen struggled in muddy conditions during the drawn opener. England batted first and were dismissed for 95 while Australia nearly doubled the score with 182. Lord's became the third Test venue in England while the home side continued the tradition of home ground authorities selecting the team. England's Edmund Peate took 6 for 85 bowling Australia out for 229 and setting up an innings and 5 run victory. Allan Steel scored his second Test century (148) out of a home total of 379. The Oval contest proved a run feast with William Murdoch scoring the first double century in Test cricket in Australia's 551, the first time a side had scored more than 500 in a Test innings (no declarations were allowed). Murdoch and Henry Scott (102) put on a record partnership for any wicket of 207 while Percy McDonnell (103) also made a century. For the first time, the entire England side bowled while the best figures were achieved by the wicketkeeper, the Rt Hon. Alfred Lyttleton with 4 for 19 from underarm lobs. England's Read batting at number 10 made 117 as the match was drawn.

NEWSPAPER HEADLINE

England Triumphs Again!

THE SCOREBOARD

FIRST TEST: 10–12 July,1884 (Old Trafford)
Match Drawn
England 95 and 9 for 180,
Australia 182

SECOND TEST: 21–23 July (Lord's)
England won by an innings and 5 runs
Australia 229 and 145,
England 379

THIRD TEST: 11–13 August (The Oval)
Match Drawn
Australia 551,
England 346 and 2 for 85

FACEBOOK MOMENT

WL Murdoch became the first sub-fielder to take a catch (off Henry 'Tup' Scott) while fielding for the opposition.

FOR THE RECORD

Most Runs:	WL Murdoch (AUS) 266
Most Wickets:	GE Palmer (AUS) 14
Highest Score:	WL Murdoch (AUS) 211 (Third Test)
Best Bowling:	G Ulyett (ENG) 7 for 36 (Second Test)
Most Catches:	WG Grace (ENG) 4
Highest Run	WL Murdoch/HJH Scott (AUS) 207
Partnership:	(Third Test, 3rd wicket)

Centuries:	**England**	**Australia**
	AG Steel	WL Murdoch
	WW Read	HJH Scott
		PS McDonnell

TWITTER FACT

WG Grace took a catch from the first ball he wicket kept to in a Test match off Alfred Lyttleton (WE Midwinter 30).

DID YOU KNOW?

Stanley Christopherson, former President of the MCC from 1939–46, played his only Test at Lord's in 1884, scoring 17 and taking 1 for 52 in the first innings.

1884–85
IN AUSTRALIA

AUSTRALIA	V	ENGLAND
W MURDOCH		A SHREWSBURY
WON	DRAWN	WON
2		3

The first of a five Test series between the two countries saw Australia troubled by internal disputes and under full-strength. Despite this it was a close-fought contest. Adelaide hosted its first Test match although violent dust storms interrupted play. Percy McDonnell's became the first batsman to score hundreds in successive Test innings, although England won the match by eight wickets with the help of 134 by William Barnes and eight wickets by left-arm spinner Bobby Peel. The Australian side for the Second Test at Melbourne saw nine debutantes and eleven changes as those playing in the first Test demanded fifty percent of the gate money. Despite Arthur Jarvis' first innings of 82, England won by ten wickets. For the Third Test in Sydney four of Australia's First Test side agreed to play. Fred Spofforth returned, taking ten wickets for the match and ensuring Australia's narrow 6 run victory, at the time the smallest winning margin. George Bonnor's century in the Fourth Test (128) in just 100 minutes and England caught on a drying wicket on the third day ensured that Australia levelled the series. England won the final Test after making 386 in response to Australia's capitulation of 163 in the first innings. Victory in the end was comprehensive, by an innings and 98 runs.

NEWSPAPER HEADLINE

England Wins Close Series

THE SCOREBOARD

FIRST TEST: 12–16 December (Adelaide)
England won by 8 wickets
Australia 243 and 191
England 369 and 2 for 67

SECOND TEST: 1–5 January (Melbourne)
England won by 10 wickets
England 401
Australia 279 and 126

THIRD TEST: 20–24 February (Sydney)
Australia won by 6 runs
Australia 181 and 165
England 133 and 207

FOURTH TEST: 14–17 March (Sydney)
Australia won by 8 wickets
England 269 and 77
Australia 309 and 2 for 38

FIFTH TEST: 21– 25 March (Melbourne)
England won by an innings and 98 runs
Australia 163 and 125
England 386

FACEBOOK MOMENT

A major pay dispute that saw wholesale changes to the Australian side almost gifted the England the Second Test and a 2–0 lead in the series.

FOR THE RECORD

Most Runs:	W Barnes (ENG) 369
Most Wickets:	W Barnes (ENG), F Spofforth (AUS) 19
Highest Score:	W Barnes (ENG) 134 (First Test)
Best Bowling:	W Barnes (ENG) 6 for 31 (Second Test)
Most Catches:	W Barnes (ENG) 8
Highest Run	W Barnes/WH Scotton (ENG) 175
Partnership:	(First Test, 3rd wicket)

Centuries:

England	**Australia**
W Barnes	P McDonnell
A Shrewsbury	GJ O'Connor
J Briggs	

TWITTER FACT

Jack Blackham's run of playing in each of the first 17 Tests for Australia ended during the Second Test at Melbourne due to a pay dispute.

DID YOU KNOW?

Five of Australia's debutantes in the Second Test – Alfred Marr, Sam Morris, Harry Musgrove, Roland Pope and Digger Robertson – never played for their country again.

1886
IN ENGLAND

ENGLAND	v	AUSTRALIA
AG STEEL		HJH SCOTT
WON	DRAWN	WON
3		0

1886 witnessed a three Test series where England dominated at home. Australia, with veterans Fred Spofforth, Joey Palmer and Tom Garrett all close to the end of their careers and missing William Murdoch, Tom Horan, Percy McDonnell, Alec Bannerman and Hugh Massie. Henry 'Tup' Scott became the first Victorian to captain Australia in this series … not surprising, perhaps, given the tour was organised by the Melbourne Cricket Club rather than private individuals. Things looked positive for the Australians in the First Test at Old Trafford when they found themselves just 18 runs short after the first innings. The visitors then collapsed to be all out for 123 in its second innings and England reached the small total six wickets down, hanging on through Richard Barlow's dourness in scoring 30. With the benefit of Arthur Shrewbury's 164 at Lord's and WG Grace's 170 at The Oval, the home side won the last two Tests of the series by an innings margin. Grace's ton helped England's to its highest score in Test cricket. Garrett bowled 99 (four ball) overs during the final Test while England's George Lohmann, in just his third Test appearance, took 12 wickets as the weather dealt cruelly with the Australians.

NEWSPAPER HEADLINE

England Dominates Weary Aussies

THE SCOREBOARD

FIRST TEST: 5–7 July (Old Trafford)
England won by 4 wickets
Australia 205 and 123
England 223 and 6 for 107

SECOND TEST: 19–21 July (Lord's)
England won by an innings and 106 runs
England 353
Australia 121 and 126

THIRD TEST: 12–14 August (The Oval)
England won by an innings and 217 runs.
England 434
Australia 68 and 149

FACEBOOK MOMENT

Lancashire's Johnny Briggs took 11 for 74 to destroy Australia in the Second Test at Lord's with his wily use of left-arm orthodox bowling.

FOR THE RECORD

Most Runs:	A Shrewsbury (ENG) 243
Most Wickets:	J Briggs (ENG) 17
Highest Score:	WG Grace (ENG) 170 (Third Test)
Best Bowling:	GA Lohmann (ENG) 7 for 36 (Third Test)
Most Catches:	WG Grace (ENG) 8
Highest Run	WG Grace/WH Scotton (ENG) 170
Partnership:	(Third Test, 1st wicket)
Centuries:	**England**
	WG Grace A Shrewsbury

WG GRACE, ENGLAND

TWITTER FACT

A crowd of 15,663 turned up to watch the second day of the Lord's Test.

DID YOU KNOW?

When Arthur Shrewsbury scored 164 at Lord's, he became the first England captain to score a Test century.

1886–87
IN AUSTRALIA

AUSTRALIA	v	ENGLAND
PS MCDONNELL		A SHREWSBURY
WON	DRAWN	WON
0		2

Despite an altercation between Australia's new captain Percy McDonnell and England's all rounder William Barnes that saw the latter out of action for the rest of the tour (Barnes threw a punch intended for the Aussie skipper's face and instead struck a brick wall), England cruised to a 2–0 series win after a tight fought initial contest. Australia's fast-medium bowling duo Charlie 'Terror' Turner and Jack Ferris often took advantage of each other's footprints at the other end to forge a feared and successful partnership. Despite preparing a fresh pitch for each side, no batsman scored a half century in the series. After McDonnell sent England into bat, and thus becoming the first captain to do so, debutantes Turner and Ferris bowled the visitors out for 45. England recovered to score 184 in the second innings and Barnes helped bowl Australia out for 97 leading to a 13 run win. In the Second Test, England recruited the services of Lancashire's Reginald Wood who was playing first class cricket for Victoria at the time. Rain delayed the start of play but Ferris and Turner again combined to bowl England out for 151. The Australians couldn't cope with the medium pace of George Lohmann, however, who became the first Test bowler to take 8 wickets in an innings. Not only did England's William Gunn play in the match but he also filled in as umpire on the final morning when Swift was absent.

NEWSPAPER HEADLINE

England Victorious but Aussie Bowlers Shine

THE SCOREBOARD

FIRST TEST: 28–31 January (Sydney)
England won by 13 runs
England 45 and 184
Australia 119 and 97

SECOND TEST: 25 February–1 March (Sydney)
England won by 71 runs
England 151 and 154
Australia 84 and 150

FACEBOOK MOMENT

Australia's debut bowlers Turner and Ferris took 35 of the
40 English wickets to fall in the two Test series.

FOR THE RECORD

Most Runs:	H Moses (AUS) 116
Most Wickets:	JJ Ferris (AUS) 18
Highest Score:	RG Barlow (ENG) 42 not out (Second Test)
Best Bowling:	G Lohmann (ENG) 8 for 35 (Second Test)
Most Catches:	W Gunn (ENG) 4
Highest Run Partnership:	RG Barlow/W Flowers (ENG) 57 (Second Test, 8th wicket)
Centuries:	Nil

TWITTER FACT

Charles Bannerman, the scorer of the first Test century at Melbourne
in 1877, made his first appearance as an umpire in Ashes cricket.

1887–88
IN AUSTRALIA

AUSTRALIA	V	ENGLAND
PS McDONNELL		WW READ
WON	DRAWN	WON
O		1

A one-off Test match in Sydney resulted in the two English sides touring Australia at the time, combining to take on Australia. England contained seven of Shrewbury's, team six of which were professionals and two of Vernon's, including the captain WW Read. Australia's second innings of 42 on a rain-affected pitch (there was no play on the second and the third days of the match) is still their lowest total in a home Test. Patrick McShane made a pair courtesy of Peel as Australia succumbed to 82 in its second innings. Lohmann and Peel took nine wickets each for the match while Australia's CTB Turner and JJ Ferris took 12 and six wickets respectively. England stretched its winning sequence to seven.

NEWSPAPER HEADLINE

Combined England Takes Ashes

THE SCOREBOARD

FIRST TEST: 10–15 February (Sydney)
England won by 126 runs.
England 113 and 137
Australia 42 and 82

FACEBOOK MOMENT

This match attracted the smallest crowd (2000) of any Test match in Australia.

NEWSPAPER HEADLINE

Two Parties, One Ashes Victory!

FOR THE RECORD

Most Runs:	A Shrewsbury (ENG)45
Most Wickets:	CTB Turner (AUS) 12
Highest Score:	A Shrewsbury (ENG) 44
Best Bowling:	CTB Turner (AUS) 7 for 43
Most Catches:	A Shrewsbury (ENG) 6
Highest Run Partnership:	A Shrewsbury/W Newham (ENG) 31 (6th wicket)
Centuries:	Nil

TWITTER FACT

England's Andrew Stoddart, who went on to captain his country in cricket and rugby, made his Test debut in the 1887–88 match.

DID YOU KNOW?

Two England teams toured Australia this summer. One was led by Arthur Shrewsbury and included future Hollywood star Charles Aubrey Smith, the other by the Hon MB (later Lord) Hawke and George Vernon.

1888

IN ENGLAND

ENGLAND	v	AUSTRALIA
AG STEEL (1) WG GRACE (2,3)		PS McDONNELL
WON	DRAWN	WON
2		1

The absence of four leading players affected Australia's Ashes chances with Spofforth, Murdoch, Jones and Giffen unable to tour. Turner and Ferris helped make up for the shortfall taking 534 wickets between them. All three of the Test matches were over in two days with one completed before lunch on the second day. Alec Bannerman made a pair in his First Test at Lord's as Australia was routed for 116 and 60. It was worse for the home side which was dealing with a muddy pitch and was bowled out for 53 and 62. On the second day, 27 wickets fell for 157 runs in just over three hours (WG Grace was one of the few to hold out, making 24). England turned the tables at The Oval under the leadership of WG Grace. The England team was selected by the home club's committee which named five Surrey players – Shuter, Read, Abel, Lohmann and Wood. Australia collapsed to be 7 for 50 by lunch. England's first innings of 317, helped by Lohmann striking the ball in ferocious fashion for an undefeated 62, proved too much for the visitors who lost by an innings and 137 runs. Heavy downpours before the match produced a soft surface that gave the side batting first an advantage. England's 172 was helped by the steadying hand of Grace (38) at the top of the order. Warmer conditions on the second day helped produce a sticky wicket to which the Australians had no answer. Five of its top seven batsmen made duck in the second innings and Australia lost by an innings and 21 runs.

NEWSPAPER HEADLINE

England Wins Rain-Affected Series

THE SCOREBOARD

FIRST TEST: 16–17 July (Lord's)
Australia won by 61 runs
Australia 116 and 60
England 53 and 62

SECOND TEST: 13–14 August (The Oval)
England won by an innings and 137 runs
Australia 80 and 100
England 317

THIRD TEST: 30–31 August (Old Trafford)
England won by an innings and 21 runs
England 172
Australia 81 and 70.

FACEBOOK MOMENT

At Old Trafford, Charlie Turner took his sixth consecutive, five wicket hauls in a Test innings (5 for 86).

FOR THE RECORD

Most Runs:	W Barnes (ENG) 90
Most Wickets:	R Peel (ENG) 24
Highest Score:	R Abel (ENG) 70 (Second Test)
Best Bowling:	R Peel (ENG) 7 for 31 (Third Test)
Most Catches:	WG Grace (ENG), GA Lohmann (ENG) 8
Highest Run Partnership:	R Abel/W Barnes (ENG) 112 (Second Test, 5th wicket)
Centuries:	Nil

TWITTER FACT

The Third Test at Old Trafford is the shortest Ashes Test on record, consuming just six hours and 34 minutes of playing time.

DID YOU KNOW?

The compulsory margin for a 'follow-on' in 1888 was 80 runs, forcing Australia to follow-on the final Test of the series at Old Trafford even though they were just 91 runs in arrears of England's first innings total.

CHAPTER 2

THE 1890s

1890
IN ENGLAND

ENGLAND	v	AUSTRALIA
WG GRACE		WL MURDOCH
WON	DRAWN	WON
2		0

England continued its dominance over Australia despite the decision of three star players – Stoddart, Peel and Ulyett – to play for their counties instead in the Second Test. WL Murdoch returned as captain after premature retirement, making him the skipper of four Australian touring teams to England. Australia began the series well with Lyons making 55 in 45 minutes (a record 36 minutes to reach his 50). The visitors failed to make the most of the bright start, however, losing seven wickets for 23 to be all out for 132. The England innings began sensationally when WG Grace was caught and bowled Turner second ball. JM Read and Ulyett rescued the home side by adding 73 before Lyons dismissed both of them. Barrett playing in his first Test match carried his bat to 67 in Australia's second innings. England made the required 137 runs for just three wickets. Grace atoned for his first innings duck and scored an undefeated 75. England's 'Nutty' Martin, a left-arm fast bowler, debuted during the Second Test at the Oval taking 12 for 102 as 22 wickets fell for 197 runs on the opening day (rain before the start of play had produced a wet wicket). In response to Australia's first innings total of 92, England again lost Grace for a duck – caught Trumble bowled Ferris. W Gunn steadied the ship and the home side finished with an eight run first innings lead. England scraped home by two wickets after Australia was again bowled out cheaply (102) in its second innings. The Third Test at Old Trafford was washed out without a ball being bowled.

NEWSPAPER HEADLINE

England Too Strong Again

THE SCOREBOARD

FIRST TEST: 22–23 July (Lord's) 1890
England won by 7 wickets
Australia 132 and 176
England 173 and 3 for 137.

SECOND TEST: 11–12 August (The Oval)
England won by 2 wickets
Australia 92 and 102
England 100 and 95

FACEBOOK MOMENT

The selectors picked Tasmanian batsman Ken Burn as the reserve wicketkeeper although he had never kept wicket in his life. He only revealed this when the Australian touring party was in the Red Sea. He played two Tests batting at number eleven, scoring 0 and 19 in the First Test. He was promoted up the order to number six in the Second Test and scored 7 and 15.

FOR THE RECORD

Most Runs:	JJ Lyons (AUS) 122
Most Wickets:	JJ Ferris (AUS) 13
Highest Score:	WG Grace (ENG) 75 (First Test)
Best Bowling:	F Martin (ENG) 6 for 50 (Second Test)
Most Catches:	H Trumble (AUS) 4
Highest Run Partnership:	WG Grace/JM Read (ENG) 74 (First Test, 2nd wicket)
Centuries:	Nil

AUSTRALIA, 1890

TWITTER FACT

WG Grace was dismissed for the first time for ducks in consecutive first innings of Tests in the 1890 Ashes.

DID YOU KNOW?

Australia's 'lucky pick' Ken Burn died in 1956 at the age of 92. At the time, he lived longer than any other Test cricketer and was a former Test cricketer for 66 years, creating another record.

1891–92
IN AUSTRALIA

AUSTRALIA	v	ENGLAND
J BLACKHAM		WG GRACE
WON	DRAWN	WON
2		1

Six ball overs were introduced for the three Test series that WG Grace debuted on Australian soil. Given the financial failure of the previous tour and Australia's lack of success against England the game had diminished in popularity. Lord Sheffield organised the tour with Grace as captain and later provided the Sheffield Shield for domestic cricket in Australia. In the First Test at Melbourne, William Bruce scored a maiden half century (57) helped by the plodding batting of AC Bannerman (45). Australia scored 240 but were outstripped by England's 264 which featured an even 50 by WG Grace. More than 20,000 watched the first two days and 10,000 the next two. England failed to chase down the home side's target of 260 with Turner taking another five wicket haul. At Sydney, Bobby Abel was the first England opener to carry his bat when making 136 out of 307 in response to Australia's 144 when Lohmann managed to take 8 for 58 off 43 overs. JJ Lyons (134) and AC Bannerman added 174 runs while the latter batted the entire third day for 67. Stoddart's 67 was not enough for the visitors who lost by 72 runs. Inspired by Australia's ability to mount a large total and the perfect batting conditions the English side accumulated 499 in its first innings at Adelaide, Stoddart stole the show with 134 and Grace contributed another half century (58). Torrential rain ended the second day early changing the pitch to a bowler's paradise. Australia was bowled out for 100 and 169 with Briggs taking 12 of the 18 wickets to fall on the Third day.

NEWSPAPER HEADLINE

Australia Regains Ashes!

THE SCOREBOARD

FIRST TEST: 1–6 January (Melbourne)

Australia won by 54 runs

Australia 240 and 236

England 264 and 158

SECOND TEST: 29 January–3 February (Sydney)

Australia won by 72 runs

Australia 144 and 391

England 307 and 156

THIRD TEST: 24–28 March (Adelaide)

England won by an innings and 230 runs

England 499

Australia 100 and 169

FACEBOOK MOMENT

Australia won the Ashes for the first time after defeating England at the SCG in the Second Test of the 1891–92 series.

FOR THE RECORD

Most Runs:	JJ Lyons (AUS) 287
Most Wickets:	J Briggs (ENG) 17
Highest Score:	JJ Lyons (AUS) 134 (Second Test)
	AE Stoddart (ENG) 134 (Third Test)
Best Bowling:	GA Lohmann (ENG) 8 for 58 (Second Test)
Most Catches:	WG Grace (ENG) 9
Highest Run	AC Bannerman/JJ Lyons (AUS) 174
Partnership:	(Second Test)

Centuries:

England	Australia
R Abel	JJ Lyons
	AE Stoddart

TWITTER FACT

Australia's opening bowler RW McLeod was unable to bowl in the second innings. He returned to Melbourne after hearing of the death of his brother.

DID YOU KNOW?

William Attewell was the first batsman to make a 'king pair' of ducks in an Ashes Test when he was bowled by Trott and caught and bowled by Giffen in the Second Test at the SCG.

1893
IN ENGLAND

AUSTRALIA	V	ENGLAND
JM BLACKHAM		AE STODDART (1)
		WG GRACE (2-3)

WON	DRAWN	WON
0	2	1

Harry Graham scored a century on debut as Australia finished 65 runs in arrears in the first innings at Lord's. England posted an historic declaration in the second innings but it was all for nowt as rain intervened after lunch on the third day. Despite being demoted to number seven in the batting order, Jackson scored a ton in the Second Test as England made 483. All-rounder George Giffen displayed perseverance on a flat track, taking 7 for 128. Australia were routed for 91 in the first innings, with Harry Trott (92) surpassing that score after the follow on, but Johnny Brigg's ten wickets in the match proved the difference. Yorkshire refused to release players from county duty for the final Test but Tom Richardson's five wickets on debut limited Australia to 204. England began poorly, losing Stoddart run out without scoring, before Gunn's only Test century secured a 39 run lead. Richardson took 10 wickets in the drawn match after Australia set England an impossible 198 in just over 2 hours.

NEWSPAPER HEADLINE

England Too Strong at Home

THE SCOREBOARD

FIRST TEST: 17–19 July (Lord's)
Match Drawn
England 334 and 8 dec. for 234
Australia 269

SECOND TEST: 14–16 August (The Oval)
England won by an innings and 43 runs
England 483
Australia 91 and 349

THIRD TEST: 24–26 August (Old Trafford)
Match Drawn
Australia 204 and 236
England 243 and 4 for 118

FACEBOOK MOMENT

This series was decided in three, three-day Test matches. In the
First Test at Lord's, rain prevented play after lunch on the third
day, resulting in an historic declaration and a draw.

FOR THE RECORD

Most Runs:	A Shrewsbury (ENG) 284
Most Wickets:	J Briggs (ENG), G Giffen (AUS) 16
Highest Score:	H Graham (AUS) 107 (First Test)
Best Bowling:	G Giffen (AUS) 7 for 128 (Second Test)
Most Catches:	WW Read (ENG), G Giffen (AUS) 4
Highest Run Partnership:	A Shrewsbury/W Gunn (ENG) 152 (First Test, 2nd wicket)

Centuries:	**England**	**Australia**
	A Shrewsbury	H Graham
	FS Jackson	
	W Gunn	

1894–95
IN AUSTRALIA

AUSTRALIA	V	ENGLAND
JM BLACKHAM (1) G GIFFEN (2–5)		AE STODDART
WON	**DRAWN**	**WON**
2		3

Test cricket had turned the corner in Australia. For the first time both Melbourne and Sydney officials promoted an English touring side. After accumulating 586 in its first innings (G Giffen 161, SE Gregory 201) Australia was caught on a sticky wicket in the second innings and lost the SCG opener by ten runs. England's Peel took advantage of the wet conditions taking 6 for 67. It was the first time a team following on had won a Test. After rolling England for 75 at the MCG (Arthur Coningham took MacLaren's wicket with his first ball and the first ball of the match), Australia stumbled to 123. England amassed 475 with Stoddart's 173 becoming the highest Test score by an Englishman proving too much. Adelaide brought a reversal of fortune with an Australian win by 328 runs. The English side struggled with the extreme heat (155 degrees F in direct sun) and were subject to allegations of excessive drinking. Albert Trott on debut scored 110 runs across two innings without being dismissed and also bowled unchanged throughout England's second innings taking 8 for 43. Australia again dictated terms at Sydney with Harry Graham's first innings century (completing the rare double of a hundred in his first Test innings in England and Australia). Rain ruined the pitch and England was bowled out for 65 and 72. Turner became the first Australian to take 100 wickets as England lost 17 wickets in just under three hours on the third day. In Melbourne, Australia's foundation of 414 was closely matched by England's 384. MacLaren scored the first of his five centuries against Australia with

120 while Peel made up for his Adelaide pair with 73. Richardson's 6 for 104 helped limit Australia's second innings to 267 with ten of the Australians reaching double figures. It wasn't enough ... JT Brown scored 140 (his century coming up in just 95 minutes) with Ward's 93 securing England's six wicket victory.

NEWSPAPER HEADLINE

England Wins Thrilling Series!

THE SCOREBOARD

FIRST TEST: 14–20 December (Sydney)
England won by 10 runs
Australia 586 and 166
England 325 and 437

SECOND TEST: 29 December–3 January (Melbourne)
England won by 94 runs
England 75 and 475
Australia 123 and 333

THIRD TEST: 11–15 January (Adelaide)
Australia won by 382 runs
Australia 238 and 411
England 124 and 143

FOURTH TEST: 1–4 February (Sydney)
Australia won by an innings and 147 runs
Australia 284
England 65 and 72

FIFTH TEST: 1–6 March (Melbourne)
England won by 6 wickets
Australia 414 and 267
England 385 and 298

FACEBOOK MOMENT

Australian George Giffen's all-round performance of 475 runs and 34 wickets remains the best in an Ashes series.

FOR THE RECORD

Most Runs:	G Giffen (AUS) 475
Most Wickets:	G Giffen (AUS) 34
Highest Score:	SE Gregory (AUS) 201 (First Test)
Best Bowling:	R Peel (ENG) 6 for 67 (First Test)
Most Catches:	R Peel (ENG), GH Trott (AUS),
	G Giffen (AUS), FA Iredale (AUS) 6
Highest Run	A Ward/JT Brown (ENG) 210
Partnership:	(Fifth Test, 3rd Wicket)

Centuries:

England	**Australia**
JT Brown	G Giffen
AC MacLaren	H Graham
A Stoddart	SE Gregory
A Ward	FA Iredale

TWITTER FACT

Australia's Syd Gregory, scorer of his country's first double century, was born at the SCG, where his Dad Ned was the curator.

DID YOU KNOW?

AE Trott, who played his third and final match for Australia in the Fifth Test, later played twice for England against South Africa!

1896
IN ENGLAND

ENGLAND	V	AUSTRALIA
WG GRACE		GHS TROTT
WON	DRAWN	WON
2		1

A record crowd of 30,000 crammed into Lord's for the First Test as Tom Richardson's six for 39 bowled the Australians out for 53. Richardson's pace was too much for the visitors with Darling's 22 the highest score. The boisterous crowd saw Grace score his 1000th run in Test cricket as England breezed to 233 for eight at stumps. Trott (143) and Gregory (103) put on 221 in 161 minutes to help Australia to 347. Rain caused England to fight for their win by six wickets. Brown's 36 considered a fighting knock in the conditions. Frank Iredale's 108 provided the perfect platform for Australia's first innings at Old Trafford. Richardson's pace (7 for 168) again caused problems as the visitors fell from 2 for 242 to be bowled for 412. KS Ranjitsinhji (Ranji) scored a debut century, undefeated on 154 but couldn't stop an Australian win. Giffen's double of 86 runs and four wickets meant he reached 1000 runs and 100 wickets in his second to last Test. A dispute over match fees saw five English players threaten to boycott the deciding Test at The Oval. Eventually it was only Gunn and Lohmann who refused to play. In a low scoring affair, it was Ranji who again starred this time in the field running out Iredale who put on 75 with Joe Darling in 45 minutes in Australia's first innings. They collapsed to be all out for 145. Eventually Australia was set 110 on a worn pitch and were routed for a 44. Peel ended his Test career with 6 for 23.

NEWSPAPER HEADLINE

Australia is 'Ranjied!'

THE SCOREBOARD

FIRST TEST: 22–24 June (Lord's)
England won by 6 wickets
Australia 53 and 347
England 292 and 111

SECOND TEST: 16–18 July (Old Trafford)
Australia won by 3 wickets
Australia 412 and 125
England 231 and 305

THIRD TEST: 10–12 August (The Oval)
England won by 66 runs
England 145 and 84
Australia 119 and 44

FACEBOOK MOMENT

Australia's captain GHS Trott (a postman by trade) had only one game off during the tour of England and played all eleven games in the US and New Zealand on the way home.

FOR THE RECORD

Most Runs:	KS Ranjitsinhji (ENG) 235
Most Wickets:	T Richardson (ENG) 24
Highest Score:	KS Ranjitsinhji (ENG) 154 (Second Test)
Best Bowling:	T Richardson (ENG) 7 for 168 (Second Test)
Most Catches:	GHS Trott (AUS), H Trumble (AUS) 5
Highest Run Partnership:	GHS Trott/SE Gregory (AUS) 221 (First Test, 4th wicket)

Centuries:

England	Australia
KS Ranjitsinhji	GHS Trott
	SE Gregory
	FA Iredale

TWITTER FACT

Jack Harry was first picked as Australia's second keeper but was then replaced before the tour sailed, he was paid £160 compensation.

DID YOU KNOW?

The Australian side played a number of matches in America on the way home and then more games in New Zealand.

1897–98
IN AUSTRALIA

AUSTRALIA	v	ENGLAND
GHS TROTT		AC MACLAREN (1–2,5)
		A STODDART (3–4)
WON	**DRAWN**	**WON**
4		1

England's touring captain Andrew Stoddart withdrew from the First Test after the death of his mother (the England players wore black armbands as a sign of respect). Archie MacLaren, Stoddart's replacement, scored 109 in England's massive first innings total of 551. Remarkably, wicketkeeper Kelly kept his slate clean throughout the innings for no byes. 'Ranji', despite an illness, managed 175 while Australia succumbed to 237 at the hands of JT Hearne. Darling became the first left hander to score a century in a Test match while Clem Hill came close with 96. Set 95 to win, England achieved the target with one wicket down but it would be their last success of the Test summer. Australia reversed its form in the Second Test after CE McLeod led the Australian charge with 112. England were still 55 runs short after two innings, on what was a fast deteriorating wicket, the highest score coming from Ranji (71). 'Monty' Noble debuted for Australia, taking six second innings wickets. Another large first innings total by the Australians at Adelaide, led by Joe Darling's 178, Iredale's 84 and Hill's 81, saw Australia bat into the third day, reaching 573. England struggled with injuries and dropped catches and were dismissed for 278 and 282. Twenty-year-old Clem Hill led the way in the Fourth Test of the summer with 188. Australia was 6 for 58, indicating that Hill's innings was one of great stamina and maturity. JT Hearne's medium-pacers took six for 98 as Australia made its way to 323. Hot conditions and nearby bushfires added to the discomfort for the visitors who again had trouble with the Australian attack. England followed-on for the third time running and Australia won the Melbourne clash by eight wickets. Stoddart dropped himself for the final Test of the series but it made little difference. Joe Darling became the first batsman to score three Test hundreds in the same series, finishing with 160 as Australia easily chased down the England target with six wickets in hand. Tom Richardson's 8 for 94 in Australia's first innings represented a strong end to his Test career.

NEWSPAPER HEADLINE

Aussies Win Ashes with Ease!

THE SCOREBOARD

FIRST TEST: 13–17 December (Sydney)
England won by 9 wickets
England 551 and 1 for 96
Australia 237 and 408

SECOND TEST: 1–5 January (Melbourne)
Australia won by an innings and 55 runs
Australia 520
England 315 and 150

THIRD TEST: 14–19 January (Adelaide)
Australia won by an innings and 13 runs
Australia 573
England 278 and 282

FOURTH TEST: 29 January–2 February (Melbourne)
Australia won by 8 wickets
Australia 323 and two for 115
England 174 and 263

FIFTH TEST: 26 February–2 March (Sydney)
Australia won by 6 wickets
England 335 and 178
Australia 239 and 276

FACEBOOK MOMENT

Joe Darling scored his third Test century with a six, whereby he hit
the ball not just over the fence but out of the ground. It was the first
six in an Ashes match scored without overthrows.

FOR THE RECORD

Most Runs:	J Darling (AUS) 537
Most Wickets:	E Jones (AUS), T Richardson (ENG) 22
Highest Score:	C Hill (AUS) 188 (Fourth Test)
Best Bowling:	T Richardson (ENG) 8 for 94 (Fifth Test)
Most Catches:	H Trumble (AUS) 8
Highest Run	J Darling/J Worrall (AUS) 193
Partnership:	(Fifth Test, 3rd wicket)

Centuries:

England	**Australia**
AC MacLaren (2)	J Darling (3)
KS Ranjitsinhji	C Hill
	C McLeod

TWITTER FACT

Australia's emphatic 4–1 Ashes win was met with such euphoria it
is said to have helped the country move a step closer to Federation.

DID YOU KNOW?

Ernie Jones, who was the first player to be no balled for 'throwing' in a
Test match, reportedly once bowled a ball through WG Grace's beard!
Jones reportedly said to Grace, "Sorry Doc, she slipped!"

1899
IN ENGLAND

ENGLAND	v	AUSTRALIA
WG GRACE (1) AS MACLAREN (2–5)		J DARLING
WON	DRAWN	WON
0	4	1

The first five Test series played in England saw one of the strongest Australia sides under Joe Darling. Victor Trumper was omitted from the original touring party but later included (on a half-share profit basis, later altered to full share), The First Test at Trent Bridge was the first time the venue had been used for a Test match, making it England's fourth ground to do so. WG Grace aged 50 played his final Test scoring 28 and 1. Wilfred Rhodes debuted taking seven wickets (Victor Trumper also debuted in this match beginning with a duck). Despite the historical milestones the match was a draw with Ranji again proving a foil for Australia scoring 42 and an undefeated 93. The Lord's Test saw the only result of the rubber with Hill adding 135 to his First Test success and Trumper making a chanceless 135. Ernie Jones took ten wickets for the match returning his best Test figures. Jones' first innings haul of seven wickets included Fry, MacLaren, Ranji and Tydesley in a devastating spell that caused the home side to collapse to 6 for 66. A wet wicket greeted the Australians at Leeds' debut as a Test ground. Darling elected to bat but Australia was soon 3 for 0. The visitors recovered to score 172 and 224, with MA Noble and SE Gregory each scoring a pair of ducks. Hearne took a hat-trick in the second innings. England at none for 19 needed 158 more runs when the rain set in. Another draw at Manchester, England's TW Hayward made a fine century (130) ensuring his side made a substantial first innings total of 372. Noble made up for the previous Test by becoming the only batsman to score separate 50s on the same

day, making an undefeated 60 and 89. A run feast ensured at The
Oval with England's 576, the highest total in a Test in England.
SE Gregory's 117 proved he could play English conditions while
WH Lockwood's off cutters proved a challenge for the Australians as
he took 7 for 71. Sadly, Clem Hill missed more than half the tour due
to illness.

NEWSPAPER HEADLINE

One Test Decides Ashes – for Australia

THE SCOREBOARD

FIRST TEST: 1–3 June (Nottingham)
Match Drawn
Australia 252 and 230
England 193 and 155

SECOND TEST: 15–17 June
Australia won by 10 wickets
England 206 and 240
Australia 421 and 0 for 28.

THIRD TEST: 29 June–1 July (Leeds)
Match Drawn
Australia 172 and 244
England 220 and 0 for 19

FOURTH TEST: 17–19 July (Manchester)
Match Drawn
England 372 and 3 for 94
Australia 196 and 346

FIFTH TEST: 14–16 August (The Oval)
Match Drawn
England 576
Australia 352 and 254

FACEBOOK MOMENT

Jack Hearne's hat-trick in the Third Test was of the highest calibre. It included the wickets of Hill, Gregory and Noble, all for ducks.

FOR THE RECORD

Most Runs:	TW Hayward (ENG) 413
Most Wickets:	E Jones (AUS) 26
Highest Score:	TW Hayward (ENG) 137 (Fourth Test)
Best Bowling:	E Jones (AUS) 7 for 88 (Second Test)
Most Catches:	KS Ranjitsinhji (ENG) 8
Highest Run Partnership:	FS Jackson/TW Hayward (ENG) 185 (Fifth Test, 1st wicket)

Centuries:	**England**	**Australia**
	TW Hayward	C Hill
	FS Jackson	V Trumper
		SE Gregory

TWITTER FACT

A new 'follow-on' rule of 120 runs was introduced for this match only.

DID YOU KNOW?

The life of England's WH Lockwood, considered something of a 'rough diamond', was enveloped by sadness. A narrow escape with a shark, and the tragic death of his wife and one of his children, eventually led him down the road of alcoholism.

CHAPTER 3

THE 1900s

1901–02
IN AUSTRALIA

AUSTRALIA	V	ENGLAND
J DARLING (1–2) H TRUMBLE (3–5)		AC MACLAREN
WON	**DRAWN**	**WON**
4		1

AC MacLaren led a weaker England side to Australia after the MCC withdrew its offer to send a representative team. Ranji, Fry, Jackson, Rhodes and Hirst were all unavailable (the latter two as Yorkshire wouldn't let them go). Nonetheless the visitors took the early honours winning at Sydney by an innings and 24 runs. The English captain reached the four-century mark with 116 while Sydney Barnes who had been plucked from the obscurity of Lancashire League cricket took five wickets in Australia's first innings. A rain-affected pitch saw Barnes capture 13 wickets in the Melbourne Test with Noble finishing with 7 for 17 in the first innings when England was skittled for 61. Reg Duff and Warwick Armstrong were held back down the order managing to score 104 and 45 not out respectively. Clem Hill made the first 99 in Test cricket while Trumble completed Australia's victory with a hat-trick (Jones, Gunn and Barnes). When Barnes had to withdraw from the Adelaide with an injured knee England was dealt a killer blow. They lost the Adelaide Test despite scoring 388 in the first innings. Hill's run in the 90s continued with 98 in the first innings and 97 in the second. England led on the first innings at the Fourth Test at Sydney, helped by MacLaren's 92. JV Saunders on debut took nine wickets but was unavailable (fractured collarbone) for the next match while JJ Kelly became the first stumper to take eight dismissals in a match. Hill's 87 in the Fifth Test at Melbourne saw his unfortunate luck continue – he was dismissed for 87. Despite this he became the first player to score 500 in a series without hitting a ton. After a loss in the first Test, Australia won the remaining four Tests.

NEWSPAPER HEADLINE

Australia's Convincing Series Win

THE SCOREBOARD

FIRST TEST: 13–16 December (Sydney)
England won by an innings and 124 runs
England 464
Australia 168 and 172

SECOND TEST: 1–4 January (Melbourne)
Australia won by 229 runs
Australia 112 and 353
England 61 and 175

THIRD TEST: 17–23 January (Adelaide)
Australia won by 4 wickets
England 388 and 247
Australia 321 315

FOURTH TEST: 14–18 February (Sydney)
Australia won by 7 wickets
England 317 and 99
Australia 299 and 121

FIFTH TEST: 28 February–4 March (Melbourne)
Australia won by 32 runs
Australia 144 and 255
England 189 and 178

FACEBOOK MOMENT

After taking 19 wickets in the first Two Tests, relatively unknown Syd Barnes was injured in the Third Test at Adelaide, ruling him out for the rest of the tour.

FOR THE RECORD

Most Runs:	C Hill (AUS) 521
Most Wickets:	MA Noble (AUS) 32
Highest Score:	AC MacLaren (ENG) 116 (First Test)
Best Bowling:	MA Noble (AUS) 7 for 17 (Second Test)
Most Catches:	LC Braund 12
Highest Run Partnership:	AC MacLaren/TW Hayward (AUS) 154 (Third Test, 1st wicket)

Centuries:	**England**	**Australia**
	AC MacLaren	RA Duff
	LC Braund	

TWITTER FACT

Australia's bowling duo of Noble and Trumble took 60 wickets in the series displaying the effectiveness of swing bowling in Australia.

DID YOU KNOW?

Australia's Reggie Duff scored a century on debut batting at number 10 in the second innings of the rain-affected Fourth Test.

1902
IN ENGLAND

AUSTRALIA	v	ENGLAND
J DARLING		AC MacLAREN
WON	DRAWN	WON
2	2	1

This was one of the strongest Ashes series to date, although the first two Tests were spoiled by rain. At Edgbaston, England's strong batting team (each player had scored a first-class century) managed 376 after a shaky start. JT Tydesley scored a masterful 138 while Australia was dismissed for 36 in the first innings but managed to play out time in the second at 2 for 46. England were two for none at Lord's with Fry and Ranji both out for ducks. MacLaren and FS Jackson led the recovery but rain but brought a premature end to the match. Australia's skipper Joe Darling made a pair (c Braund b Barnes) in the only ever Test at Bramall Lane Sheffield while Australia won by 143 runs. Barnes returning to the side after early success on the previous Australia tour took six first innings wickets while Clem Hill further established his reputation with a second innings century (113). Australia's 3–run victory at Old Trafford began with a Victor Trumper century before lunch on the first day. Darling returned to form with 51, including two sixes hit out of the ground. FS Jackson's 128 helped England even the honours before bowling the visitors out for a measly 86 as Lockwood took his wicket count to eleven for the match. The Australian captain was dropped by Fred Tate on 16, when he went on to make 37. England needed 124 but fell perilously close when Tate was bowled by Saunders. Hill's diving one-handed catch to dismiss Lilley on the boundary was one for the ages. The Oval Test known as 'Jessop's match' for his batting heroics. Chasing 263 to win England slumped to 5 for 48 before Jessop intervened scoring the fastest century in Test cricket in just 75 minutes. Trumble bowled unchanged through the match taking 12 wickets. Rhodes and Hirst scored the runs to win the match, although not in singles as the Neville Cardus inspired legend goes.

NEWSPAPER HEADLINE

Australia Takes Tight Series

THE SCOREBOARD

FIRST TEST: 29–31 May (Edgbaston)
Match Drawn
England 9 for 376
Australia 36* and 2 for 46 *Ashes record

SECOND TEST: 12–14 June (Lord's)
Match Drawn
England 2 for 102

THIRD TEST: 3–5 July (Bramall Lane)
Australia won by 143 runs
Australia 194
England 145 and 195

FOURTH TEST: 24–26 July (Old Trafford)
Australia won by 3 runs
Australia 229 and 86
England 262 and 120

FIFTH TEST: 11–13 August (The Oval)
England won by 1 wicket
Australia 324 and 121
England 183 and 9for 263

FACEBOOK MOMENT

Sussex off spinner Fred Tate was marked never to play for England again after dropping a crucial catch and being dismissed with four runs to win the vital Fourth Test.

FOR THE RECORD

Most Runs:	FS Jackson (ENG) 308
Most Wickets:	H Trumble (AUS) 26
Highest Score:	JT Tyldesley (ENG) 138 (First Test)
Best Bowling:	H Trumble (AUS) 8 for 65 (Fifth Test)
Most Catches:	LC Braund (ENG) 8
Highest Run	FS Jackson/LC Braund (ENG) 141
Partnership:	(Fourth Test, 6th wicket)

Centuries:

England	**Australia**
FS Jackson	C Hill
JT Tyldesley	V Trumper
AC MacLaren	
G Jessop	

TWITTER FACT

Tailender Wilfred Rhodes – who later opened the batting for England – topped the English averages at 67.

DID YOU KNOW?

Hugh Trumble's haul of 8 for 65 and 4 for 108 as well as undefeated scores of 64 and 7 made him the first Australian to score a 50 and take ten wickets in a Test match.

1903–04
IN AUSTRALIA

AUSTRALIA	v	ENGLAND
MA NOBLE		PF WARNER
WON	DRAWN	WON
2		3

The 1903–04 series marked the first time that the MCC chose and managed the touring team. AC MacLaren had been asked by the Australians to bring a team but declined when Barnes and Lockwood made themselves unavailable. The visitors were led by Pelham 'Plum' Warner who revived the Ashes legend by his tour book, *How we recovered the Ashes.* England won the high scoring opening encounter at the SCG. 'Monty' Noble on debut as captain scored his only Test ton (133) while England responded with 577 including RE Foster's 287 in his first Test. He became the first batsman to share in three century partnerships in one innings, putting on 130 with Rhodes for the tenth wicket stand. Trumper's second innings 185, the highlight of Australia's innings. When Clem Hill was given run out the crowd showed its disapproval, while Warner came close to taking his players from the field. The catching on both sides was poor as England's strong first innings of 315 set itself up for victory after heavy rain interrupted play. Both sides were bowled out cheaply in the second innings with Rhodes taking 15 wickets for the match. England's 2–0 status was partly reversed with the help of a first innings Trumper century and Gregory's ton in the second. BJT Bosanquet's use of googlies captured seven wickets for the match but it wasn't enough. Australia won by 216 runs. Rain again affected the Fourth Test at Sydney, with a day's play lost due to rain. England managed 210 on a wet wicket with newcomer 'Tibby' Cotter taking six wickets. Australia was then routed by googly bowler Bosanquet. At one stage, he took 5 for 12 as Australia was bowled out for 133. With Hayward absent ill, England was rolled for 101 with Hugh Trumble doing most of the damage taking 7 for 28 including a hat-trick for the second time.

NEWSPAPER HEADLINE

Australia Too Late as England Win Series

THE SCOREBOARD

FIRST TEST: 11–17 December (Sydney)
England won by 5 wickets
Australia 285 and 485
England 577 and 194

SECOND TEST: 1–5 January (Melbourne)
England won by 185 runs
England 315 and 103
Australia 122 and 111

THIRD TEST: 15–20 January (Adelaide)
Australia won by 216 runs.
Australia 388 and 345
England 245 and 278

FOURTH TEST: 26 February–3 March (Sydney)
England won by 157 runs
England 249 and 210
Australia 131 and 171

FIFTH TEST: 5–8 March (Melbourne)
Australia won by 218 runs
Australia 247 and 133
England 61 and 101

FACEBOOK MOMENT

With his first ball in Test cricket, Ted Arnold dismissed Victor Trumper in the first innings of the First Test at Sydney.

FOR THE RECORD

Most Runs:	V Trumper (AUS) 574
Most Wickets:	W Rhodes (ENG) 31
Highest Score:	REW Foster (ENG) 287 (First Test)
Best Bowling:	W Rhodes (ENG) 8 for 68 (Second Test)
Most Catches:	LC Braund (ENG) 9
Highest Run	RE Foster/LC Braund (ENG) 192
Partnership:	(First Test, 5th wicket)

Centuries:	**England**	**Australia**
	RE Foster	V Trumper (2)
	LC Braund	MA Noble
		SE Gregory

TWITTER FACT

Wilfred Rhodes took 15 wickets in the Second Test, despite suffering eight dropped catches.

DID YOU KNOW?

Australia's sling bowler Albert 'Tibby' Cotter, later to perish at Bersheeba during WWI while serving with the Australian Light Horse, debuted in the Fourth Test.

1905
IN ENGLAND

ENGLAND	V	AUSTRALIA
FS JACKSON		J DARLING
WON	DRAWN	WON
2	3	0

A disappointing tour for Australia's batsmen in which Joe Darling led the side again, the same year the Australian Board of Control emerged. England batsman FS Jackson, the former Fagmaster of Winston Churchill's at Harrow captain England. Jackson returned to big cricket, after serving in the Boer War. Jackson won all five tosses during the Test matches as England marched to a comfortable victory. JT Bosanquet's googlies again caused trouble for the Australians taking eight second innings wickets in the First Test at Trent Bridge. AC MacLaren's 140 was his fifth hundred of his Test career. The Lord's Test was again rain interrupted, as was the Leeds Test, resulting in draws. Jackson scored an undefeated century in the latter while Tyldesley posted his second hundred against Australia despite the leg theory of Armstrong and the off theory of McLeod (where bowlers bowl to a particular side of the wicket and pack that part of the field with fieldsmen). Arnold Warren took six wickets including Trumper twice, but never played for England again. Jackson scored his second century in a row at Old Trafford, where Australia was bowled out for under two hundred in each innings. J Darling (73) and RA Duff (60) provided the only real resistance for Australia. CB Fry and JT Tyldesely shone at The Oval with 144 and 112 respectively while RA Duff helped Australia assemble a strong first innings total of 363. Australia's Tibby Cotter showed promise with seven first innings wickets from 40 overs.

NEWSPAPER HEADLINE

England Far Too Strong

THE SCOREBOARD

FIRST TEST: 29–31 May (Trent Bridge)
England won by 213 runs
England 196 and 426
Australia 221 and 188

SECOND TEST: 15–17 June (Lord's)
Match Drawn
England 282 and 5 for 151
Australia 181

THIRD TEST: 3–5 July (Leeds)
England won by an innings and 80 runs
England 301 and 295
Australia 195 and 224

FOURTH TEST: 24–26 July (Old Trafford)
Match Drawn
England 446
Australia 197 and 169

FIFTH TEST: 14–16 August (The Oval)
Match Drawn
England 430 and 6 dec. for 261
Australia 363 and 124

FACEBOOK MOMENT

1905 became known as Jackson's Year after he led the batting averages with 70 and bowling averages with 17. All the while leading his side to victory.

FOR THE RECORD

Most Runs:	FS Jackson (ENG) 492
Most Wickets:	F Laver (AUS), W Armstrong (AUS) 16
Highest Score:	RA Duff (AUS) 146 (Fifth Test)
Best Bowling:	A Cotter (AUS) 7 for 148 (Fifth Test)
Most Catches:	W Rhodes (ENG) 6
Highest Run	JT Tyldesley/RH Spooner (ENG) 158
Partnership:	(Fifth Test, 6th wicket)

Centuries:

England	**Australia**
CB Fry	RA Duff
FS Jackson (2)	AC MacLaren
JT Tyldesley (2)	

TWITTER FACT

Warwick Armstrong scored 2002 runs and took 130 wickets in all matches on the 1905 tour.

DID YOU KNOW?

The respective captains Darling and Jackson were born on the same day, 21 November 1870, and died within fifteen months of each other. Darling became a Tasmanian Member of Parliament while Jackson was the English Governor in Bengal during his career as a diplomat.

1907–08
IN AUSTRALIA

AUSTRALIA	V	ENGLAND
MA NOBLE		FL FANE (1–3)
		AO JONES (4–5)
WON	DRAWN	WON
4		1

England's Frederick Lane took over captaincy duties for the first three Tests when AE Jones, the nominated skipper was ruled out for an illness that almost developed into pneumonia. George Gunn who happened to be in Australia for health reasons scored 119 and 74 in the First Test eventually scoring in the series 462 runs at 51. Australia won the series opener by two wickets at the SCG, with fill-in England skipper Fane criticised for under-bowling Crawford, who could make the ball break back on the most even of wickets, and Rhodes. Jack Hobbs debuted at Melbourne scoring 83 in the first innings as England scored 382. KL Hutchings playing in just his second Test made 126 in England's first innings. GR Hazlitt had a chance for a run-out but threw inaccurately as Barnes and Fielder scampered home to win by one wicket. Adelaide delivered its traditional high temperatures as the players sweltered in above 100°F. RJ Hartigan managed a century on debut adding 243 in even time. England's bowlers were let down by poor catching from the visitors. Jack O'Connor's eight wicket debut helped Australia to a 245-run win. Trumper registered a pair at the MCG as Australia waltzed to a 308-run win helped by England's collapse from 1 for 69 to all out 105 after rain intervened. Hobbs hit ten boundaries in his 70-minute score of 57. WW Armstrong mad his first hundred in Ashes cricket as Saunders followed up his five first innings wickets with four more, as England in pursuit of 495 capitulated for 186. Sent in to bat in the final Test at the SCG, Australia collapsed to be all out for 137, Barnes' making most of the damp conditions capturing 7 for 60. Gunn's undefeated 122 helped England to accumulate 281. Making up for the previous Test, Trumper batted for 241 minutes scoring an undefeated 166. Crawford had again shown his effectiveness taking eight wickets for the match. Despite resistance from Rhodes and Fane, England's chase fell 49 runs short.

NEWSPAPER HEADLINE

Australia Too Good At Home

THE SCOREBOARD

FIRST TEST: 13–19 December (SCG)
Australia won by 2 wickets
England 273 and 300
Australia 300 and 8 for 275

SECOND TEST: 1–7 January (Melbourne)
England won by 1 wicket
Australia 266 and 397
England 382 and 9 for 282

THIRD TEST: 10–16 January (Adelaide)
Australia won by 245 runs
Australia 285 and 506
England 363 and 183

FOURTH TEST: 7–11 February (Melbourne)
Australia won by 308 runs
Australia 214 and 385
England 105 and 186

FIFTH TEST: 21–27 February (Sydney)
Australia won by 49 runs
Australia 137 and 422
England 281 and 229

FACEBOOK MOMENT

Financial problems, late withdrawals, illness on tour and lack of variety shackled England's Ashes defence.

FOR THE RECORD

Most Runs:	G Gunn (ENG) 462
Most Wickets:	JV Saunders (AUS) 31
Highest Score:	VT Trumper (AUS) 166 (Fifth Test)
Best Bowling:	S Barnes (ENG) 7 for 60 (Fifth Test)
Most Catches:	LC Braund (ENG), KL Hutchings (ENG), 8
Highest Run Partnership:	RJ Hartigan/C Hill (AUS) 243 (Third Test, 8th wicket)

Centuries:

England	Australia
G Gunn (2)	WW Armstrong
KL Hutchings	MJ Hartigan
	C Hill
	VT Trumper

TWITTER FACT

Trumper's 166 at Sydney saw him become the second batsman after Clem Hill to pass 2000 Test runs.

DID YOU KNOW?

England captain Fred Fane later read his own premature obituary published in Wisden. He was also the first Ireland-born player to score a Test hundred for England.

1909

IN ENGLAND

ENGLAND	V	AUSTRALIA
MA NOBLE		AC MACLAREN
WON	DRAWN	WON
1	2	2

Australia defeated England in a convincing manner in the Test series as well as having the better of the drawn matches. Unbeaten for more than three months, the Australian side was often under rated by the English press. England's selection policy was one of a revolving door with no less than 25 players called upon. The home side won the First Test at Edgbaston by ten wickets, after Blythe and Hirst blitzed Australia out for 74, a first innings score from which they never recovered. Lord's was the turning point of the series when VS Ransford's undefeated 143 and W Armstrong's six second innings wickets ensured a nine wicket win for the visitors. England's JH King in his only Test top scored in his side's first innings with 60. CG Macartney's slow left-armers achieved 11 wickets at Leeds where Australia again dominated. England's Gilbert Jessop strained his back so badly, after just 70 minutes play that he was out for the remainder of the season. Frank Laver's 8 for 31 ripped England out for 119 in the drawn encounter at Old Trafford, earning him the best analysis by a tourist in Tests in England. A lack of centuries was corrected when Warren Bardsley scored 136 and 130 becoming the first to make a century in each innings of a Test match. Everton footballer Jack Sharp also scored a ton. Douglas Carr took seven wickets in his only Test for England, after appearing in County cricket for the first time for Kent aged 37. He took three early wickets but was then over-bowled for the rest of the match.

NEWSPAPER HEADLINE

Aussies Take Rubber, 2–1

THE SCOREBOARD

FIRST TEST: 27–29 May (Edgbaston)
England won by 10 wickets
Australia 74 and 151
England 121 and 105

SECOND TEST: 14–16 June (Lord's)
Australia won by 9 wickets
England 269 and 121
Australia 350 and 1 for 41

THIRD TEST: 1–3 July (Leeds)
Australia won by 126 runs
Australia 188 and 207
England 182 and 87

FOURTH TEST: 26–28 July (Old Trafford)
Match Drawn
Australia 147 and 279
119 and 108

FIFTH TEST: 9–11 August (The Oval)
Match Drawn
Australia 325 and 5 dec. 339
England 352 and 3 for 104

FACEBOOK MOMENT

England's Oval Test match debutant Frank Woolley had to wait 19
minutes to receive his first delivery. Warwick Armstrong spent the
time bowling trial balls, that were permitted at the start of a spell.

FOR THE RECORD

Most Runs:	W Bardsley (AUS) 396
Most Wickets:	Colin Blythe (ENG) 18
Highest Score:	Vernon Ransford (AUS) 143 not out (Second Test)
Best Bowling:	Frank Laver (AUS) 8 for 31 (Fourth Test)
Most Catches:	W Armstrong (AUS), AC MacLaren (ENG) 7
Highest Run Partnership:	SE Gregory/W Bardsley (AUS) 180 (Fifth Test, 1st wicket)

Centuries:

England	Australia
J Sharp	W Bardsley (2)
	VS Ransford

TWITTER FACT

Australia's Monty Noble won the toss in each of the Test matches just as FS Jackson did for the home side in 1905.

DID YOU KNOW?

Warren Bardsley scored twin centuries in the final Test at the Oval but had to wait 17 years to make another Test ton in England.

1911–12
IN AUSTRALIA

AUSTRALIA	v	ENGLAND
C HILL		JWHT DOUGLAS
WON	DRAWN	WON
1		4

England dominated the Australian summer despite the setback of losing its captain Pelham Warner with illness to all five Tests. JWHT Douglas, 1908 middleweight Olympic boxing champ and amateur England representative, led the side. Early signs were good for Australia with a Trumper century while Dr HV Hordern's googlies 12 wickets helped Australia's win by 146 runs. Douglas' decision not to open the bowling with Barnes was widely criticised. At age 38 Barnes' opening spell at the MCG had Australia reeling at 4 for 11. Twenty-year-old JW Hearne in just his second Test scored 114 as England managed 265 in response to Australia's 184. FR Foster's second innings, six wickets and Hobbs undefeated 126 resulted in an England victory by eight wickets. The dose was repeated at Adelaide where Hobbs continued his form with 187. Hill managed 98, his fifth score between 96 and 99 against England. Barnes took eight wickets for the match. Hobbs and Rhodes put on 323 for the opening stand at Melbourne as England climbed to 589 in response to Australia's first innings of 191. Douglas took five wickets as the home side lost wickets at a steady rate and were bowled out for 173. The final Test of the summer marked the end of Trumper and Hill's Test careers, with the former finishing with a 50, while the third and sixth day of the match were lost to rain. Hordern took ten wickets for the match as the googly continued to reign supreme. England however again won, this time by 70 runs. In the bloodletting after the series loss, Hill came to blows with a selector in the boardroom and six prominent players stood aside for the 1912 tour of England.

NEWSPAPER HEADLINE

England Regains Ashes

THE SCOREBOARD

FIRST TEST: 15–21 December (Sydney)
Australia won by 146 runs
Australia 447 and 308
England 318 and 291

SECOND TEST: 30 December–3 January (Melbourne)
England won by 8 wickets
Australia 184 and 299
England 265 and 2 for 219

THIRD TEST: 12–17 January (Adelaide Oval)
England won by 7 wickets
Australia 133 and 476
England 501 and 3 for 112

FOURTH TEST: 9–13 February (Melbourne)
England won by an innings and 225 runs
Australia 191 and 173
England 589

FIFTH TEST: 23 February–1 March (Sydney)
England won by 70 runs
England 324 and 214
Australia 176 and 292

FACEBOOK MOMENT

Syd Barnes took five wickets for six runs in his opening spell of the Second Test at Melbourne setting England up for victory and a psychological advantage over Australia for the series.

FOR THE RECORD

Most Runs:	JB Hobbs (ENG) 662
Most Wickets:	SF Barnes (ENG) 34
Highest Score:	JB Hobbs (ENG) 187 (Third Test)
Best Bowling:	Dr HV Hordern (ENG) 7 for 90 (First Test)
Most Catches:	C Hill (AUS) 8
Highest Run Partnership:	JB Hobbs/W Rhodes (ENG) 323 (Fourth Test, 1st wicket)

Centuries:	**England**	**Australia**
	JB Hobbs (3)	V Trumper
	JW Hearne	
	W Rhodes	
	FE Woolley	

TWITTER FACT

Despite not playing in any of the Test matches due to illness Pelham Warner wrote in Wisden, … 'it is something to have taken two teams to Australia that have returned unconquered.'

DID YOU KNOW?

England captain JWHT Douglas was nicknamed 'Johnny Won't Hit Today' after he scored only 33 in more than three hours of batting against Victoria.

1912
IN ENGLAND

ENGLAND	V	AUSTRALIA
CB FRY		SE GREGORY
WON	DRAWN	WON
1	2	0

The Ashes were included in this Triangular tournament involving England, Australia and South Africa. 'The Big Six' (Hill, Trumper, Armstrong, Cotter, Carter and Ransford) declined to tour after disagreeing over the choice of team manager picked by the Board of Control. Australia's side was effectively a second eleven. The Lord's Test lost half of the first day and the majority of the second when rain intervened. Hobbs opened with 107 in England's total of 310. Australia replied with 282, while CG Macartney was dismissed for 99 in the drawn opener. Rain ruined the Second Test at Old Trafford. Australia's Bill Whitty dismissed the first three English batsmen, Hobbs, Rhodes and Spooner finishing with 4 for 43. Rhodes continued his good form opening with 92. The victor of the Third Test at The Oval was declared the winner of the tournament. It was the home side by 244 runs in the first timeless Test played in England Whitty again starred with seven wickets for the match, as did GR Hazlitt with 7 for 25 in England's second innings. Hobbs, Woolley and Fry all scored 50s in this low scoring affair. Woolley also became the third player to score a half century and take ten wickets for the match. It was captain Syd Gregory's 52nd and last Test against England.

NEWSPAPER HEADLINE

England Win Troubled Series

THE SCOREBOARD

FIRST TEST: 24–26 June (Lord's)
Match Drawn
England 7 for 310
Australia 7 for 282

SECOND TEST: 29–31 July (Old Trafford)
Match Drawn
England 203
Australia 0 for 14

THIRD TEST: 19–22 August (The Oval)
England won by 244 runs
England 245 and 175
Australia 111 and 65

FACEBOOK MOMENT

In the Third and deciding Test at The Oval, Australia lost nine wickets for 19 as they were dismissed for a paltry 65 in the second innings.

FOR THE RECORD

Most Runs:	JB Hobbs (ENG) 224
Most Wickets:	GR Hazlitt (AUS), WJ Whitty (AUS) 12
Highest Score:	JB Hobbs (ENG) 107 (Third Test)
Best Bowling:	GR Hazlitt (AUS) 7 for 25 (Third Test)
Most Catches:	GR Hazlitt (AUS) 12
Highest Run	C Kelleway/C G Macartney (AUS) 146
Partnership:	(First Test, 2nd wicket)
Centuries:	**England**
	JB Hobbs

TWITTER FACT

Australia's star batsman for the past decade Victor Trumper died of Bright's Disease just three years later, on 28 June 1915, aged 37.

DID YOU KNOW?

Rain completely spoiled the Second Test. Play began at 3 o'clock on the first day, at 5 o'clock on the second and the third day was a washout.

CHAPTER 4

THE 1920s

1920–21
IN AUSTRALIA

AUSTRALIA	v	ENGLAND
WW ARMSTRONG		JWHT DOUGLAS
WON	DRAWN	WON
5		0

Having declined an invitation to tour Australia in 1919–20 for fear that it had not had time to regain its pre-war standard, England was whitewashed 5–0 in the first post-war series played. It was the first result of its kind in Ashes history and was not repeated until the 2006–07 series. England was unlucky to come up against a powerful Australian team led in an uncompromising fashion by Warwick Armstrong. The Australia captain, having ballooned to twenty stone in weight, was able to use genuine pace bowlers Jack Gregory and Ted McDonald as well as leg spinner Arthur Mailey in attack. Australia consistently accumulated large totals, due to a very strong batting line-up including Macartney, Armstrong and Collins. Australia's second innings 581 in the First Test at Sydney featured Herbie Collins 104 (at the age of 32) and Armstrong, 158 in his first Test as captain. England succumbed to 190 and 281, with the wickets shared between Kelleway (4), Gregory (6) and Mailey (6). Hobbs revived former glories with a century on a sticky wicket in Melbourne but couldn't stop another landslide loss. Australia's first innings 499 replete with maiden centuries from CE Pellew and Jack Gregory was too much for England to match. The Adelaide Oval pitch resembled a road with the match producing six centuries. England led on the first innings after CAG Russell's undefeated 135. Mailey conceded 300 in the match as Australia won back the Ashes. JWH 'Harry' Makepeace became the oldest player to score an inaugural Test hundred, in England's first innings total of 284, while Armstrong scored his second century in a row despite suffering from malaria. Macartney's chanceless 170 in the Sydney Test was witnessed by a 12-year-old Don Bradman during his first visit to a Test match.

NEWSPAPER HEADLINE

Australia's Ashes Whitewash

THE SCOREBOARD

FIRST TEST: 17–22 December (Sydney)
Australia won by 377 runs
Australia 267 and 582
England 190 and 281

SECOND TEST: 31 December–4 January (Melbourne)
Australia won by an innings and 91 runs
Australia 499
England 251 and 157

THIRD TEST: 14–20 January (Adelaide)
Australia won by 119 runs
Australia 354 and 582
England 447 and 370

FOURTH TEST: 11–16 February (Melbourne)
Australia won by 8 wickets
Australia 284 and 315
England 389 and 2 for 211

FIFTH TEST: 25 February–1 March (Sydney)
Australia won by 9 wickets
England 204 and 280
Australia 392

FACEBOOK MOMENT

England's Harry Makepeace, who once played for Everton in a winning FA Cup side, played his entire four Test career during this series, scoring a century as a 39-year-old.

FOR THE RECORD

Most Runs:	HL Collins (AUS) 557
Most Wickets:	AA Mailey (AUS) 36
Highest Score:	CG Macartney (AUS) 170 (Fifth Test)
Best Bowling:	AA Mailey (AUS) 9 for 121 (Fifth Test)
Most Catches:	JM Gregory (AUS) 15 * Ashes record
Highest Run	CG Macartney/JM Gregory (AUS) 198
Partnership:	(Fifth Test, 4th wicket)

Centuries:

England	Australia
JB Hobbs (2)	WW Armstrong (3)
JWH Makepeace	HL Collins (2)
CAG Russell	JM Gregory
	CE Kelleway (2)
	C Macartney
	CE Pellew (2)

TWITTER FACT

Leg spinner Arthur Mailey's 36 wickets for the series was an Ashes record.

DID YOU KNOW?

Australian batsman Roy Park's Test career lasted just one ball when he was bowled by Howell. Park's wife missed seeing his entire Test career when she bent over to pick up her knitting.

1921

IN ENGLAND

AUSTRALIA	V	ENGLAND
WW ARMSTRONG		JWHT DOUGLAS (1–2)
		HON LH TENNYSON (3–5)
WON	DRAWN	WON
3	2	O

England debuted 16 players throughout the series as a rampant McDonald and Gregory meant the home side suffered another devastating series defeat. The First Test was over by the second afternoon after the Aussie pace duo blasted England out for under 200 with 16 wickets between them. Percy Holmes' only Ashes Test top scored with 30 in the first innings. When debutante Ernest Tyldesley was bowled after the ball struck his face it summed up England's plight. England's six changes for the Second Test at Lord's made little difference, although Woolley's two scores in the 90s showed signs of defiance. Bardsley top scored in both Australian innings. JWHT Douglas was relieved of the English captaincy (after seven consecutive losses) while England debuted four more players. New England captain Tennyson showed bravery when he scored 63 and 36 batting virtually one-handed after injuring it in the field. Macartney's first innings 115 set the visitors up for another win, this time by 219 runs. England had the upper hand in the drawn Test at Old Trafford after CAG Russell made 101 (amazingly 81 on the leg side). Tennyson declared on the second day after the first was washed out although the players had to return to the field when Armstrong pointed out that under two-day rules the declaration was invalid. It was then that Armstrong famously bowled his second consecutive over. The final encounter was a match of farcical proportions where Armstrong protested at Test matches being limited to three days, (he read part of a newspaper in the outfield as he left his bowlers and fielders to fend for themselves). The first day was interrupted by rain as England reached 4 for 129. CP Mead's undefeated 182 with a century before lunch on the second day helped the home side to declare at 8 for 403. England's Russell scored his second consecutive Ashes hundred with 102 not out as the match was drawn. England, with the help of rain had batted the game out for the second time of the series.

NEWSPAPER HEADLINE

Australia Dominate Again

THE SCOREBOARD

FIRST TEST: 23–30 May (Trent Bridge)
Australia won by 10 wickets
England 112 and 147
Australia 232 and 0 for 30

SECOND TEST: 11–14 June (Lord's)
Australia won by 8 wickets
England 187 and 283
Australia 342 and 2 for 131

THIRD TEST: 2–5 July (Leeds)
Australia won by 219 runs
Australia 407 and 273
England 259 and 202

FOURTH TEST: 23–26 July (Old Trafford)
Match Drawn
England 4 dec. for 362 and 1 for 44
Australia 175

FIFTH TEST: 13–16 August (The Oval)
Match Drawn
England 8 dec. for 403 and 2 for 244
Australia 389

FACEBOOK MOMENT

Lionel Tennyson was made England captain for the Third Test in time to stop a record run of defeats of eight (by South Africa).

FOR THE RECORD

Most Runs:	FE Woolley (ENG) 343
Most Wickets:	EA MacDonald (AUS) 27
Highest Score:	CP Mead (ENG) 182 not out (Fifth Test)
Best Bowling:	JM Gregory (AUS) 6 for 58 (First Test)
Most Catches:	JM Gregory (AUS) 8
Highest Run Partnership:	CAG Russell/G Brown (ENG) 158 (Fifth Test, 1st wicket)

Centuries:	**England**	**Australia**
	CP Mead	C Macartney
	CA Russell (2)	

TWITTER FACT

Australia used 30 players in the series, a then record in Ashes Tests.

DID YOU KNOW?

Three of Australia's 1921 side were from the Gordon District Cricket Club in Sydney. Charlie Macartney, Bert Oldfield and Johnny Taylor were among the tourists while the manager Sydney Smith was a former Gordon player.

1924–25
IN AUSTRALIA

AUSTRALIA	v	ENGLAND
HL COLLINS		AER GILLIGAN
WON	DRAWN	WON
4		1

Eight ball overs, and the beginning of England's famous Hobbs and Sutcliffe partnerships could not stymie Australia in the summer of 1924–25. Two (unrelated) Richardsons, Arthur and Vic, as well as Bill Ponsford debuted at the SCG. Ponsford's 110 and HL Collins 114 led Australia to 450. The English openers began with partnerships of 157 and 110 as England mounted totals of 298 and 411. Hobbs a century in the first innings, Sutcliffe a century in the second. JM Taylor's 108 ensured a large second innings for Australia while England despite scoring 411 failed by 193 runs to chase the total down. Woolley avoided a pair by 123 runs. Ponsford made it two tons in two Tests with 128 at the MCG, while Vic Richardson registered his highest Test score of 138 (scoring 21 off one Douglas over) as Australia reached a record score of 600. AEV Hartkopf also made 80 on debut. Hobbs and Sutcliffe added 283, with the latter making a century in each innings. Tate took nine wickets for the match while Australia won by 81 runs. A record total of 236, 258 people attended the match. The high scoring continued at Adelaide with Jack Ryder rescuing the side from 6 for 119 to score an unconquered 210. England's attack was weakened by injuries to Tate, Gilligan and Freeman. When England went in late on the second day they changed their batting order losing debutante WW Whysall and keeper H Strudwick before stumps. Hobbs rattled up another ton batting at five, and England scored two totals in excess of 300 for the match. Set 375 to win they fell 12 short of victory. Sutcliffe became the first batsman to make four centuries

JACK HOBBS AND HERBERT SUTCLIFFE, ENGLAND

in the series setting England up for an imposing innings and 29 run win, ending Australia's run of 16 Tests without defeat. New Zealand-born leg spinner CV Grimmett took 11 wickets for the final Test as Australia bounced back to win by 307 runs. Sutcliffe having scored a triumphant 734 runs at 81 was bowled for a duck by Gregory in his final innings of the tour.

NEWSPAPER HEADLINE

Australia Win but Hobbs and Sutcliffe Star

THE SCOREBOARD

FIRST TEST: 19–27 December (SCG)
Australia won by 193 runs
Australia 450 and 452
England 298 and 411

SECOND TEST: 1–8 January (Melbourne)
Australia won by 81 runs
Australia 600 and 250
England 479 and 290

THIRD TEST: 16–23 January (Adelaide Oval)
Australia won by 11 runs
Australia 489 and 250
England 365 and 363

FOURTH TEST: 13–18 February (Melbourne)
England won by an innings and 29 runs
England 548
Australia 269 and 250

FIFTH TEST: 27 February–4 March (Sydney)
Australia won by 307 runs
Australia 295 and 325
England 167 and 146

FACEBOOK MOMENT

In the Second Test at Melbourne, eight new balls were used before Australia reached 200. The captains agreed to use Grade 3 balls for the entire first innings for both sides.

FOR THE RECORD

Most Runs:	H Sutcliffe (ENG) 734
Most Wickets:	MW Tate (ENG) 38
Highest Score:	J Ryder (AUS) 201 (Third Test)
Best Bowling:	MW Tate (ENG) 6 for 99 (Second Test)
Most Catches:	FE Woolley (ENG) 9
Highest Run Partnership:	JB Hobbs/H Sutcliffe (ENG) 283 (Second Test, 1st wicket)

Centuries:

England	Australia
JB Hobbs (3)	WH Ponsford (2)
H Sutcliffe (4)	HL Collins
FE Woolley	J Ryder
	JM Taylor
	VY Richardson

TWITTER FACT

In the Second Test, Hobbs and Sutcliffe batted through the entire day of the Test, becoming the first pair to do so.

DID YOU KNOW?

Herbie 'Lucky' Collins, a bookmaker by trade, took over the captaincy from cricket provocateur Warwick Armstrong after leading Australia against South Africa. In 1926 Collins was accused of fixing the final Test of the series.

1926
IN ENGLAND

ENGLAND	V	AUSTRALIA
AW CARR (1–4) APF CHAPMAN (5)		HL COLLINS (1–2, 4–5) W BARDSLEY (3)
WON	DRAWN	WON
0	4	1

Despite outstanding domestic seasons Alan Kippax, Vic Richardson and Charlie Kelleway missed out on selection in the Australian touring side. England won back the Ashes after 14 years with a single Test win at the Oval after the first four matches were drawn. Australia's paceman Gregory was blighted by injury and McDonald was living in Lancashire. The series opened with a drawn match and only 50 minutes of play before heavy rain at Nottingham ended the match. Notably future Australian captain Bill Woodfull made his debut. Lord's saw high scoring with four centurions across the two sides in three innings, the youngest was Patsy Hendren at 37. At age 43, Warren Bardsley carried his bat for 193 in Australia's first innings lasting 398 minutes. Another example of the limits of three days was obvious when the visitors scored 494 in their first innings at Leeds. Bardsley filling in for Collins was out first ball and then Macartney who was dropped off the fourth ball he received scored a century before lunch on the first day (Woodfull also scored his first Test ton. England slumped to 6 for 140 while Grimmett took five first innings wickets. Rain virtually wiped out the first days play at Old Trafford while Macartney's third hundred of the series and Woodfull's second saw Australia to 335. England was 5 for 305 by the end of the third day, Hobbs' 74 continuing a consistent summer after he took over the captaincy when Carr became ill. Percy Chapman replaced AW Carr as captain while Wilfred Rhodes at age 48 came back into the home side. The timeless Test witnessed a 172–opening stand from Hobbs and Sutcliffe on a rain-affected pitch in England's second innings after Australia led by 22 in the first. Mailey's leg spinners taking six wickets. Chasing 415, Australia lost Woodfull for a duck to Larwood who took six top order wickets for the match. Rhodes then spun his side to victory as Australia collapsed to be all out 125. Until the final match it was indeed a batsman's series.

NEWSPAPER HEADLINE

England: The Ashes Returned

THE SCOREBOARD

FIRST TEST: 12–15 June (Trent Bridge)
Match Drawn
England 0 for 32

SECOND TEST: 26–29 June (Lord's)
Match Drawn
Australia 383 and 5 for 194
England 475

THIRD TEST: 10–13 July (Headingley)
Match Drawn
Australia 494
England 294 and 3 for 254

FOURTH TEST: 24–27 July (Old Trafford)
Match Drawn
Australia 335
England 5 for 305

FIFTH TEST: 14–18 August (The Oval)
England won by 289 runs
England 280 and 436
Australia 302 and 125

FACEBOOK MOMENT

England's Wilfred Rhodes, at the age of 48, was recalled to the Test side for the timeless Fifth Test at the Oval, spinning England to victory with 4 for 44 in the second innings. Rhodes had played his first Test in 1899, which was WG Grace's last.

FOR THE RECORD

Most Runs:	JB Hobbs (ENG) 486	
Most Wickets:	AA Mailey (AUS) 14	
Highest Score:	W Bardsley (AUS) 193 not out (Second Test)	
Best Bowling:	AA Mailey (AUS) 6 for 138 (Fifth Test)	
Most Catches:	H Sutcliffe (ENG) 8	
Highest Run	WM Woodfull/CG Macartney (AUS) 235	
Partnership:	(Third Test, 2nd wicket)	
Centuries:	**England**	**Australia**
	JB Hobbs (2)	W Bardsley
	EH Hendren	CG Macartney (3)
	H Sutcliffe	AJ Richardson
		WM Woodfull (2)

TWITTER FACT

England's Harold Larwood, who later bowled with such devastating force in the 1932–'Bodyline' series, debuted in the Second Test at Lord's.

DID YOU KNOW?

The 1926 Australian touring side lost just one match out of the 40 played. Sadly, it turned out to be the most important match of the tour in the Fifth Test at the Oval ... thus losing the Ashes.

1928–29
IN ENGLAND

AUSTRALIA	V	ENGLAND
J RYER		P CHAPMAN
WON	DRAWN	WON
1	0	4

England retained the Ashes they won on home soil in 1926 with a 4–1 series victory in Australia. The 1928/29 series marked the debut of 20-year-old batting prodigy Don Bradman, fresh from plundering Shield attacks from around the country, but the summer was defined by England batsman Wally Hammond, playing in his first Ashes series. Hammond was poised, assured and graceful as he scored two double centuries and two centuries among the record 903 runs for the series. Bradman was dropped after Australia's disastrous First Test loss in Brisbane – by 605 runs after Chapman declined to force the follow-on – and England went on to win the next three Tests and the series. After failing in the first Test with scores of 18 and one, Bradman returned to Australia's Third Test team and went on to amass 468 runs for the series. Future 'Bodyline' captain Douglas Jardine made his top score in an Ashes Test with 98 in the Second Test at Sydney.

NEWSPAPER HEADLINE

England Retains the Ashes!

THE SCOREBOARD

FIRST TEST: 30 November–5 December (Brisbane)
England won by 675 runs
England 521 and 636
Australia 122 and 253

SECOND TEST: 14–20 December (Sydney)
England won by 8 wickets
Australia 253 and 397
England 636 and 2/16

THIRD TEST: 29 December–5 January (Melbourne)
England won by 3 wickets
Australia 397 and 368
England 417 and 7/332

FOURTH TEST: 1–8 February, 1929 (Adelaide)
England won by 12 runs
England 334 and 383
Australia 369 and 336

FIFTH TEST: 8–16 March, 1929 (Melbourne)
Australia won by 5 wickets
England 519 and 257
Australia 491 and 5/287

FACEBOOK MOMENT

Nineteen-year-old New South Welshmen Archie Jackson stroked his
way to a magnificent 164 on debut in the Fourth Test at the Adelaide
Oval, eclipsing Bradman in an innings full of wrists flicks through the
covers and exquisite footwork.

FOR THE RECORD

Most Runs:	Wally Hammond (ENG) 905
Most Wickets:	Jack White (ENG) 25
Highest Score:	Wally Hammond (ENG) 251 (Second Test)
Best Bowling:	Jack White (ENG), 8 for 126 (Fourth Test)
	*Ashes record
Most Catches:	Percy Chapman (ENG), Jack Ryder (AUS) 8
Highest Run	Wally Hammond/Douglas Jardine (ENG) 262
Partnership:	(Fourth Test, 3rd wicket)
Centuries:	**England**

England	Australia
Wally Hammond (4)	Bill Woodfull (3)
EH Hendren	Don Bradman (2)
Jack Hobbs	Archie Jackson
M Leyland	HSTL Hendry
H Sutcliffe	AF Kippax
	Jack Ryder

TWITTER FACT

All-rounder Otto Nothling replaced Don Bradman for the Second Test, and although failing to take a wicket scored 44 in the second innings. He never played for Australia again and later became a prominent Brisbane dermatologist.

DID YOU KNOW?

In 2013, complete signatures of the Australian and English sides were found in a copy of *The Pugh's Almanac* – a directory events, businesses and sundries published 1859–1927 – when England's Phil Imison inherited the dilapidated edition from his mother.

CHAPTER 5

THE 1930s

1930
IN ENGLAND

ENGLAND	V	AUSTRALIA
APF CHAPMAN (1–4) RES WYATT (5)		WM WOODFULL
WON	DRAWN	WON
1	2	2

The 1930 series marked the arrival of Don Bradman as a run
scoring force of previously unknown proportions. England won the
First Test despite Bradman's 131 and helped by Sydney Copley, a
24-year-old member of the Nottinghamshire ground staff, taking
a spectacular catch to end the McCabe/Bradman partnership. At
Lord's Bradman scored what he considered his best innings in Test
cricket, a chanceless 254 as Australia won by seven wickets. Kumar
Shri Duleepsinhji emulated his uncle KS Ranjitisinhji by scoring a
century in his first Test with 173. Bradman's 334 at Leeds included,
300 in a day and centuries before lunch and between lunch and
tea. This was the highest Test innings overtaking RE Foster's 287.
With only 45 minutes play on the third day and none on the last
day, the Fourth Test was drawn. Bradman took his Test aggregate
to 974 with a double century at the Oval while Ponsford made 110
in Australia's first innings of 695. Archie Jackson was considered to
be one of Australia's brightest shining lights despite a disappointing
series scored 73. England's opener Herb Sutcliffe's 161 and 54 weren't
enough to stave off defeat. Left-arm slow medium Percy Hornibrook
ripped through the home side taking 7 for 92. Hobbs at the age of 47
played his final Test finishing with scores of 47 and 9.

Bradman Dominates as Aussies Win Back Ashes

THE SCOREBOARD

FIRST TEST: 13–17 June (Trent Bridge)
England won by 93 runs
England 270 and 302
Australia 144 and 355

SECOND TEST: 27 June–1 July (Lord's)
Australia won by 7 wickets
England 425 and 375
Australia 6 dec. for 729 and 3 for 72

THIRD TEST: 11–15 July (Headingley)
Match Drawn
Australia 566
England 391 and 3 for 95

FOURTH TEST: 25–29 July (Old Trafford)
Match Drawn
Australia 345
England 251

FIFTH TEST: 16–22 August (The Oval)
Australia won by an innings and 39 runs
England 405 and 251
England 695

FACEBOOK MOMENT

Just weeks away from his 22nd birthday Don Bradman's 334 at Leeds marked a new high-water mark for batting in a Test match. Although the match was drawn the innings, in which Bradman was not out at the end of the first day, demonstrated the challenges England would face in the ensuing years.

FOR THE RECORD

Most Runs:	DG Bradman (AUS) 974 * Ashes record
Most Wickets:	CV Grimmett (AUS) 29
Highest Score:	DG Bradman (AUS) 334 (Third Test)
Best Bowling:	PM Hornibrook (AUS) 7 for 92 (Fifth Test)
Most Catches:	AFP Chapman (ENG) 7
Highest Run	DG Bradman/A Jackson (AUS) 243
Partnership:	(Fifth Test, 4th wicket)

Centuries:

England	Australia
APF Chapman	DG Bradman (4)
KS Duleepsinhji	SJ McCabe
WR Hammond	WH Ponsford
H Sutcliffe	WM Woodfull

TWITTER FACT

Bradman's amazing run scoring during the 1930 series inspired England cricket authorities to devise 'Bodyline' to cut the Australian batsman down to size.

DID YOU KNOW?

Australia won the final Test at The Oval on what was captain Bill Woodfull's 33rd birthday.

1932–33
IN AUSTRALIA

AUSTRALIA	V	ENGLAND
WM WOODFULL		DR JARDINE
WON	DRAWN	WON
1		4

Known as the 'Bodyline' series, the controversy arose by the England
side's use of fast short-pitched bowling (led by captain Douglas
Jardine) aimed at the batsman's chest and head with a ring of leg
side fielders. Bradman was too ill to play in the First Test at Sydney
which brought McCabe's skills to the fore. McCabe's undefeated 187
included 51 of a last wicket stand of 55 in Australia's total of 360.
England, with the help of three centuries, including the Nawab
of Pataudi, reached 524 before bowling the home side out for 164.
England won by ten wickets when they scored the solitary single
needed on the final day. Larwood took ten wickets for the match.
When Bradman did appear, he was bowled first ball by a long hop
from Bill Bowes in front of a then record crowd at the MCG of 63,993.
Australia struggled to 228 on a slow wicket with Jack Fingleton's
83 the stand out. O'Reilly's 5 for 63 off 34.3 overs saw England
dismissed for 169. Bradman batted for 185 minutes, scoring an
unconquered 103 in Australia's second innings. Another five wicket
haul from O'Reilly delivered the Test Australia's way by 111 runs.
Adelaide was the scene of the climax of hostilities as Woodfull was
struck in the chest in Australia's first innings on a fiery second
day in front of a crowd of 50, 962. When Oldfield was struck in the
head on the third day, the crowd threatened to jump the fence. The
Australian and English cricket Boards exchanged angry cables after
Woodfull's much publicised remark to the England manager that
'only one side was playing cricket'. At one stage, it looked as if the
tour may be abandoned until cooler heads prevailed. England were

too strong again at Brisbane and Eddie Paynter, suffering from acute appendicitis, struck the Ashes-winning six as England reached 4 for 162 in the second innings. Archie Jackson died of tuberculosis on the same day at the age of 23.

Bradman was again restricted to the more modest scores of 48 and 71 in Australia's Fifth Test loss. Wally Hammond's 101 and night watchman Larwood's unlikely 98 saw England surpass Australia's first innings score of 435. Richardson scored a pair as Australia limped to a second innings score of 182. Hammond slammed a six to finish to claim an eight-wicket victory.

NEWSPAPER HEADLINE

England's Bodyline too strong for Aussies

THE SCOREBOARD

FIRST TEST: 2–7 December (Sydney)
England won by 10 wickets
Australia 360 and 164
England 524

SECOND TEST: 30 December–3 January (Melbourne)
Australia won by 11 runs
Australia 228 and 191
England 169 and 139

THIRD TEST: 13–19 January (Adelaide Oval)
England won by 338 runs
England 341 and 412
Australia 222 and 193

FOURTH TEST: 10–16 February (Brisbane)
England won by 6 wickets
Australia 340 and 175
England 356 and 162

FIFTH TEST: 23–28 February (Sydney)
England won by 8 wickets
Australia 435 and 182
England 454 and 168

FACEBOOK MOMENT

After England's 338 run win at Adelaide when Australia was bowled out for 222 and 193, it was clear that Australia had little answer for the Bodyline tactics.

FOR THE RECORD

Most Runs:	H Sutcliffe (ENG), W Hammond (ENG) 440
Most Wickets:	H Larwood (ENG) 33
Highest Score:	H Sutcliffe (ENG) 194 (First Test)
Best Bowling:	H Larwood (ENG) 5 for 28 (First Test)
Most Catches:	DR Jardine (ENG) 9
Highest Run	H Sutcliffe/WR Hammond (ENG) 188
Partnership:	(Fifth Test, 2nd wicket)

Centuries:

England	Australia
WR Hammond (2)	DG Bradman
H Sutcliffe	SJ McCabe

TWITTER FACT

'Hammy' Love kept for Australia in his only Test at Brisbane. He took three catches and scored 8 runs.

DID YOU KNOW?

'Bodyline' was devised when Douglas Jardine saw footage of Bradman looking uncomfortable batting against short-pitched bowling at the Oval in 1930. Jardine leapt up and called out "I've got it. He's yellow". From there, the notion of 'leg theory' involving short pitched bowling developed.

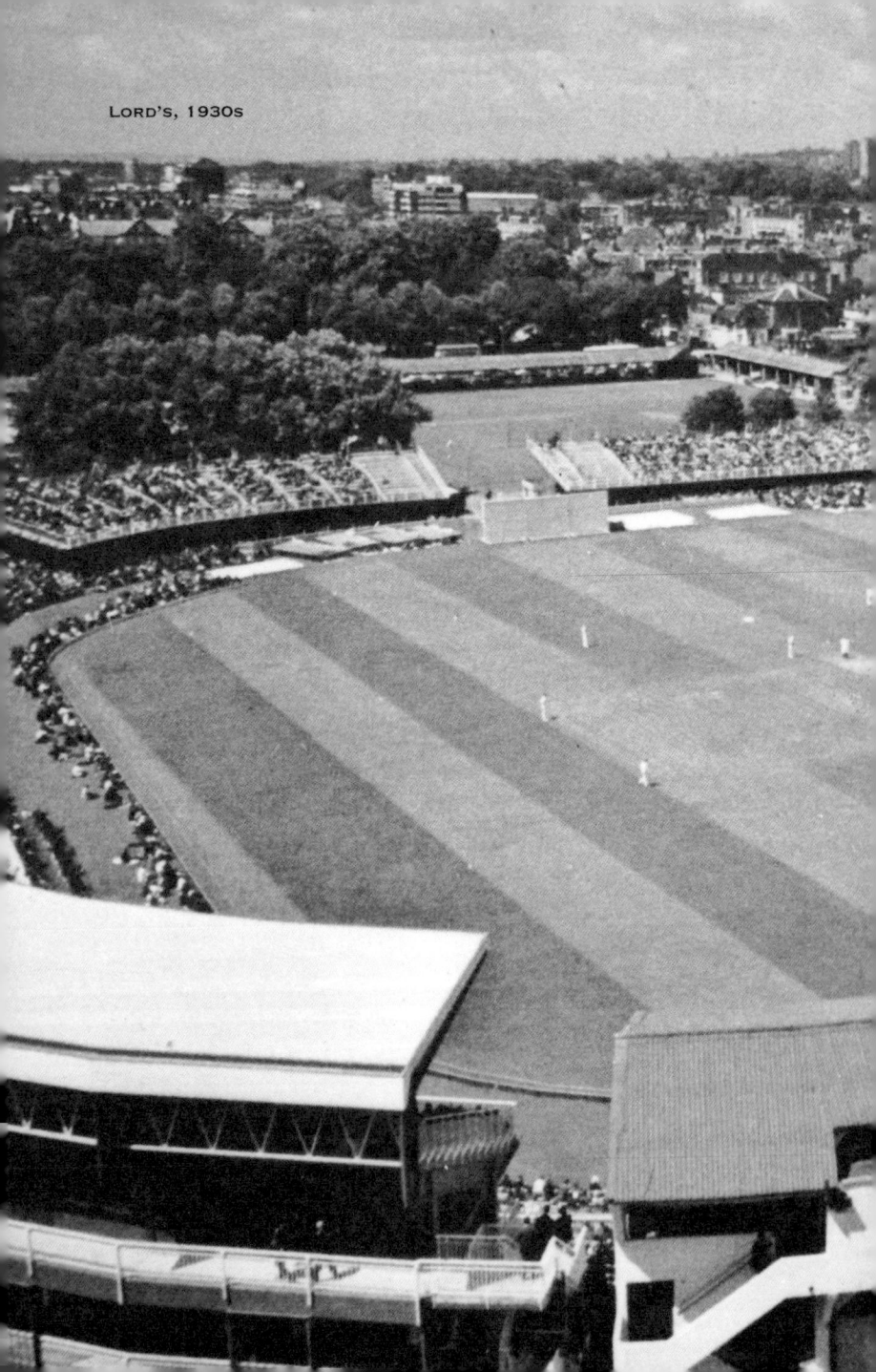

LORD'S, 1930s

1934
IN ENGLAND

ENGLAND	V	AUSTRALIA
CF WALTER (1) RES WYATT (2–5)		WH WOODFULL

WON	DRAWN	WON
1	2	2

With the MCC now fairly against the use of Bodyline, the three major figures from the 1932–33 campaign; Jardine, Larwood and Voce were missing from the 1934 series. Cyril Walters captained England in the First Test at Trent Bridge due to an injury to Bob Wyatt. Playing in his first Test Arthur Chipperfield, not out 99 at lunch was out three balls later becoming the first to do so on debut. Australia won with just ten minutes to spare with O'Reilly taking 11 wickets for the match. Lord's drew an England victory when Hedley Verity made the most of the wet pitch, taking 14 wickets for 80 on the third day. Despite O'Reilly taking three wickets (Walters, Wyatt, Hammond) in four balls England amassed 627 in its first innings at Old Trafford with Patsy Hendren (132) and Maurice Leyland (153) doing the repairs. Hendren became the second oldest batsman in the Ashes to score a ton (45 years, 151 days). Bradman, batting down the order, continued his modest form in scoring 30 while Stan McCabe made 137. Another drawn encounter at Leeds resulted after Bradman scored his second triple century. The final, timeless Test at The Oval was the 'Bradman and Ponsford' show, with the Australian pair breaking all Test records in adding 451 for the second wicket. Ponsford's 266 consumed almost eight hours in his final Test appearance while Bradman's 244 was complemented by 77 in the second innings. Woolley, who had returned to England colours at the age of 47, failed with scores of 4 and 0. England's Bill Bowes took nine wickets for the match but it was Clarrie Grimmett's leg spinners (5 for 64) that routed England for 145 in its second innings.

NEWSPAPER HEADLINE

Bradman Bats and Bats and Bats!

THE SCOREBOARD

FIRST TEST: 8–12 June (Trent Bridge)
Australia won by 238 runs
Australia 374 and 273
England 268 and 141

SECOND TEST: 22–25 June (Lord's)
England won by an innings and 38 runs
England 440
Australia 284 and 118

THIRD TEST: 6–10 July (Old Trafford)
Match Drawn
England 627
Australia 491 and 1 for 66

FOURTH TEST: 20–24 July (Headingley)
Match Drawn
England 200 and 6 for 229
Australia 584

FIFTH TEST: 18–22 August (The Oval)
Australia won by 562 runs
Australia 701 and 327
England 321 and 145

FACEBOOK MOMENT

Bradman and Ponsford's partnership of 451 at The Oval helped
Australia mount a total of 701 in its first innings.

FOR THE RECORD

Most Runs:	DG Bradman (AUS) 758
Most Wickets:	WJ O'Reilly (AUS) 28
Highest Score:	DG Bradman 304 (Fourth Test)
Best Bowling:	H Verity (ENG) 8 for 43 (Second Test)
Most Catches:	WR Hammond (ENG) 12
Highest Run	WH Ponsford/DG Bradman (AUS) 451
Partnership:	(Fifth Test, 2nd wicket) *Ashes record

Centuries:

England	**Australia**
M Leyland (3)	DG Bradman (2)
EH Hendren	WA Brown
LEG Ames	SJ McCabe
	WH Ponsford (2)

TWITTER FACT

Australia regained the Ashes for the second time on the birthday of the Australian captain Bill Woodfull, August 22nd.

DID YOU KNOW?

Australia's Hans Ebeling, later one of the organisers of the 1977 Centenary Test, made his only appearance in Test cricket at The Oval, taking 3 for 74 in the first innings.

DON BRADMAN, AUSTRALIA

1936–37
IN AUSTRALIA

AUSTRALIA	v	ENGLAND
DG BRADMAN		GOB ALLEN
WON	DRAWN	WON
3		2

Remarkably, Australia came back from 2–0 to win the series 3–2, the first in which Don Bradman captained Australia. Australia started well at the Gabba when England opener Stan Worthington was out to the first ball of the match, attempting to hook. England recovered from 3 for 20 to post 358 with Maurice Leyland scoring yet another century against Australia (126 after his three tons in the 1934 series). Fingleton scored his fourth Test century in successive innings. Australia was bowled out for 58 on a wet wicket with Allen taking 5 second innings wickets as England coasted to a 322 run win. At Sydney, Hammond scored the third of his four double centuries against Australia. Australia again batted on a wet wicket and was bowled out for 80 with Bradman registering his second duck in consecutive innings. The Australian captain's 82 in the second innings and McCabe's 93, didn't stop Australia losing by an innings and 22 runs. The Melbourne encounter attracted a record attendance of 350,535 Australia then declared, having reached 9 for 200 after rain again affected the pitch. England also declared at 9 for 76. Right-arm fast medium bowler Morris Sievers was virtually unpayable on a gluepot as the ball rose from a good length taking 5 for 21. Bradman reversed Australia's batting order holding back Fingleton, McCabe and himself until the wet pitch eased. After joining Fingleton at 5 for 97 they added 346, Bradman made 270 and Fingleton 136. England were still 365 runs short after Leyland's unbeaten 111 saw England score 323 in its second innings. Chuck Fleetwood-Smith took 5 for 124. In Adelaide, Australia was bowled out on a good wicket for 288 as the series again tilted England's way. Charlie Barnett scored a fine 129 but England collapsed and led by only 42 on the first innings. Bradman scored his second double century for Australia as Hammond took five wickets. England was bowled out for 243 with Fleetwood-Smith's six second inning wickets taking his match tally to ten. England's meagre responses of 239 and 165 (on a drying pitch) compared to Australia's first innings of 604 meant an unlikely series win to Australia.

NEWSPAPER HEADLINE

Australia's Comeback Retains Ashes

THE SCOREBOARD

FIRST TEST: 4–9 December (Brisbane)
England won by 322 runs
England 358 and 256
Australia 234 and 58

SECOND TEST: 18–22 December (Sydney)
England won by an innings and 22 runs
England 6 dec. for 427
Australia 80 and 324

THIRD TEST: 1–7 January (Melbourne)
Australia won by 365 runs
Australia 9 dec. for 200 and 564
England 9 dec. for 76 and 323

FOURTH TEST: 29 January–4 February (Adelaide Oval)
Australia won by 148 runs
Australia 288 and 433
England 330 and 243

FIFTH TEST: 26 February–3 March (Melbourne)
Australia won by an innings and 200 runs
Australia 604
England 239 and 165

FACEBOOK MOMENT

Bradman and Fingleton's 6th wicket stand of 346 enabled Australia to score 564, putting Australia in the box seat to bowl England out for 323 and turn the series.

FOR THE RECORD

Most Runs: DG Bradman (AUS) 810
Most Wickets: W Voce (ENG) 26
Highest Score: DG Bradman (AUS) 270 (Third Test)
Best Bowling: W Voce (ENG) 6 for 41 (First Test)
Most Catches: DG Bradman (SCG) 7
Highest Run   JHW Fingleton/DG Bradman (AUS) 346
Partnership: (Third Test, 6th wicket)
Centuries: **England**   **Australia**
                       C Barnett   CL Badcock
                       WR Hammond   DG Bradman (3)
                       M Leyland   JHW Fingleton (2)
                                              SJ McCabe

TWITTER FACT

More than 950,000 spectators attended the 1936–37 Ashes series, creating an all-time record.

DID YOU KNOW?

Jack Fingleton's 100 in the First Test at Brisbane saw him become the first player to score hundreds in four consecutive Test innings. After the run of success, he was out first ball in the second innings.

1938
IN ENGLAND

ENGLAND	V	AUSTRALIA
WR HAMMOND		DG BRADMAN
WON	DRAWN	WON
1	2	1

The 1938 Ashes series marked a significant revival in English cricket with the emergence of a number of younger players. Australia had difficulty replacing the likes of Woodfull, Ponsford and Kippax while the omission of Grimmett and Oldfield were likely selectors' mistakes. Bradman lost the toss in all four Tests (The Third Test at Old Trafford was abandoned because of rain without a ball being bowled). At Trent Bridge, Stan McCabe made his famous 232 in his first innings, as he scored 72 of the last 77 runs. Bradman called his players out onto the players' balcony to witness the finest innings he had ever seen. Australia's 411 was in response to England's 658 which featured tons by Barnett, Hutton, Paynter (216 not out) and a 20-year-old Denis Compton. Bradman managed to set a series record with his 13th hundred in Ashes cricket with an undefeated 144 in Australia's second innings and Bill Brown (133) batted it out for a draw. Fans at Lord's witnessed another draw and a Hammond double century (240). Bill Brown also hit a unconquered 206 in Australia's first innings while another Bradman century meant the visitors finished at 6 for 204 in the game's final innings. Australian leg spinner Bill O'Reilly –who earned the nickname Tiger on his last English tour – took ten wickets for the match at Leeds on a damp pitch. Australia won the low scoring contest by five wickets as Bradman made his third successive hundred in successive Test innings at Leeds. Len Hutton's 364 at The Oval broke Bradman's highest Test score of 334. Hutton batted for more than 13 hours as England made 7 for 903. Chuck Fleetwood-Smith's unflattering figures of 1 for 298 off 85 overs remains an Ashes record for most runs conceded. Bradman and Fingleton, due to injuries, were unable to bat and Australia capitulated for 201 and 123.

NEWSPAPER HEADLINE

England Draws Ashes Series

THE SCOREBOARD

FIRST TEST: 10–14 June (Trent Bridge)
Match Drawn
England 658
Australia 411 and 6 dec. for 627

SECOND TEST: 24–28 June (Lord's)
Match Drawn
England 494 and 8 dec. for 242
Australia 422 and 6 for 204

THIRD TEST: 8–12 July (Old Trafford)
Match abandoned without a ball being bowled

FOURTH TEST: 22–25 July (Headingley)
Australia won by 5 wickets
England 223 and 123
Australia 242 and 5 for 107

FIFTH TEST: 20–24 August (The Oval)
England won by an innings and 579 runs * Ashes record
England 7 dec. for 903 * Ashes record
Australia 201 and 123

FACEBOOK MOMENT

Australian wicketkeeper Ben Barnett missed stumping Len Hutton when he was 40. Hutton went on to make 364 and England 7 dec. for 903. His record-breaking innings set England up to win the match and draw the series.

FOR THE RECORD

Most Runs:	WA Brown (AUS) 512
Most Wickets:	WJ O'Reilly (AUS) 22
Highest Score:	L Hutton (ENG) 364 (Fifth Test)
	* Ashes record
Best Bowling:	WJ O'Reilly (AUS) 5 for 66 (Third Test)
Most Catches:	WR Hammond (ENG) 8
Highest Run	L Hutton/M Leyland (ENG) 382
Partnership:	(Fifth Test, 2nd wicket)

Centuries:

England	Australia
CJ Barnett	DG Bradman (3)
DS Compton	WA Brown (2)
WR Hammond	SJ McCabe
J Hardstaff	
L Hutton (2)	
M Leyland	
E Paynter	

TWITTER FACT

England's Denis Compton – later known as the 'Brylcream Boy' – was only 20 years and 19 days old when he scored his first Test century.

DID YOU KNOW?

Australia's Clayvel 'Jack' Badcock, despite scoring 118 in the Fifth Test of the 1936–67 Ashes, struggled to get bat on ball in the 1938 series. He failed completely in the Tests, scoring 9, 5, 0, 0, 4, 5 not out, 0 and 9.

CHAPTER 6

THE 1940s

1946–47
IN AUSTRALIA

AUSTRALIA	V	ENGLAND
DG BRADMAN		WR HAMMOND (1–4)
		NWD YARDLEY (5)
WON	DRAWN	WON
3	2	0

When Bradman was on 28 in the First Test, what seemed a legitimate catch to gully was given not out and ultimately had a decisive influence on the series. Bradman went on to score 187 adding 276 with Hassett (128) for the third wicket. Australia scored 654. England batted twice after violent storms and were routed by Miller (7 for 60) in the first innings and Toshack (6 for 82) in the second, with victory coming on the fifth day. Test matches in Australia were now limited to 30 hours. England captain Wally Hammond was clearly not the force he had been pre-war and failed again in England's 255 at Sydney. Australia replied with 659 with Bradman and Barnes both scoring 234, and adding 405 for the fifth wicket. Bill Edrich managed a second innings ton (119), Colin McCool's eight wickets for the match helped cause an innings and 33 run loss for the visitors. At Melbourne Australia was rescued in its first innings by McCool's only Test century while fast bowler Ray Lindwall also notched a ton during the first drawn Test in Australia for 65 years. Both Compton and Arthur Morris scored a century in each innings of the Adelaide Test. For Morris, it was his third Test century in consecutive innings. Bradman was bowled for a first innings duck by Alec Bedser by what he considered to be one of the best balls he faced. He narrowly missed being bowled for another duck in the second before finishing undefeated on 56. Hammond missed the Fifth Test at Sydney with fibrositis with Norman Yardley taking the helm. Hutton retired ill with tonsillitis after scoring 122 in England's first innings of 280 with Lindwall capturing seven wickets.

Right-arm leg spinner Douglas Wright's seven scalps gave England the advantage before England was bowled for 186 with McCool again making inroads, taking 5 for 44 in Australia by five wickets.

NEWSPAPER HEADLINE

Aussies win back the Ashes

THE SCOREBOARD

FIRST TEST: 29 November–4 December (Brisbane)
Australia won by an innings and 332 runs
Australia 645
England 141 and 172

SECOND TEST: 13–19 December (Sydney)
Australia won by an innings and 33 runs
England 255 and 371
Australia 8 dec. 659

THIRD TEST: 1–7 January (Melbourne)
Match Drawn
Australia 365 and 536
England 351 and 7 for 310.

FOURTH TEST: 31 January–6 February (Adelaide Oval)
Match Drawn
England 460 and 8 dec. for 340
Australia 487 and 1 for 215

FIFTH TEST: 28 February–5 March (Sydney)
Australia won by 5 wickets
Australia 280 and 186
England 253 and 5 for 214

FACEBOOK MOMENT

The England side believe they had Bradman, who had struggled to reach 28, caught at gully by Jack Ikin in the first Test at Brisbane. He was given not out and made 187 out of Australia's massive first innings total of 645. The 38-year-old Bradman went on to score 680 runs for the series.

FOR THE RECORD

Most Runs:	DG Bradman (AUS) 680
Most Wickets:	DVP Wright (ENG) 23
Highest Score:	DG Bradman (AUS), SG Barnes (AUS) 234 (Second Test)
Best Bowling:	KR Miller (AUS) 7 for 60 (First Test)
Most Catches:	WR Hammond (ENG) 6
Highest Run Partnership:	SG Barnes/DG Bradman 405 (Second Test, 5th wicket)

Centuries:	**England**	**Australia**
	DS Compton (2)	SG Barnes
	WJ Edrich	DG Bradman (2)
	L Hutton	AL Hassett
	C Washbrook	R Lindwall
		CL McCool
		AR Morris (3)

TWITTER FACT

England lost 15 wickets in under four hours on rain-affected pitch to lose the First Test at the Gabba.

DID YOU KNOW?

England's wicketkeeper Godfrey Evans batted for 97 minutes on a pair before he scored in the second innings of the Adelaide Test. He remained 10 not out.

1948
IN ENGLAND

ENGLAND	V	AUSTRALIA
NWD YARDLEY		DG BRADMAN
WON	DRAWN	WON
O	1	4

Bradman's 1948 team to England performed so well they were nicknamed 'The Invincibles' An attack consisting of Ray Lindwall, Keith Miller and Bill Johnston, as well as an experimental rule allowing a new ball every 55 overs (and the fact that England was still recovering from the loss of players during the war) saw Bradman's side return undefeated. Australia's 509 run reply to England's first innings 165 at Trent Bridge set the tone for the series. Not even Denis Compton's second innings 184 could save the home side as Australia coasted to victory by eight wickets. Australia's irascible opener Sid Barnes scored a second innings hundred at Lord's after placing a bet before the match that he would make a century (he made nought in the first innings). Lindwall's eight wickets for the match again brought England down, bowled out for 215 and 186. At Old Trafford, Compton mishit a ball from Lindwall into his head when he was 4, later retiring hurt at 33. Resuming with a head bandage and stitches Compton added 121 with Bedser before finishing with an undefeated 145. When fielding in short (a position in which he was notorious for over-reaching) Barnes was struck under the ribs. He later collapsed after batting for half an hour, retiring hurt on 1. England's first innings 496 at Leeds was helped by tons from Cyril Washbrook's and Bill Edrich. It could have been much worse for the Australians with the hosts 2 for 423 at one stage. Australia responded in kind with 19-year-old Neil Harvey making an Ashes century on debut. England declared its second innings closed and set Australia 404 to win in 345 minutes. Bradman and Arthur Morris put on a partnership of 301

Bradman's 'Invincibles' greeting King George VI, 1948

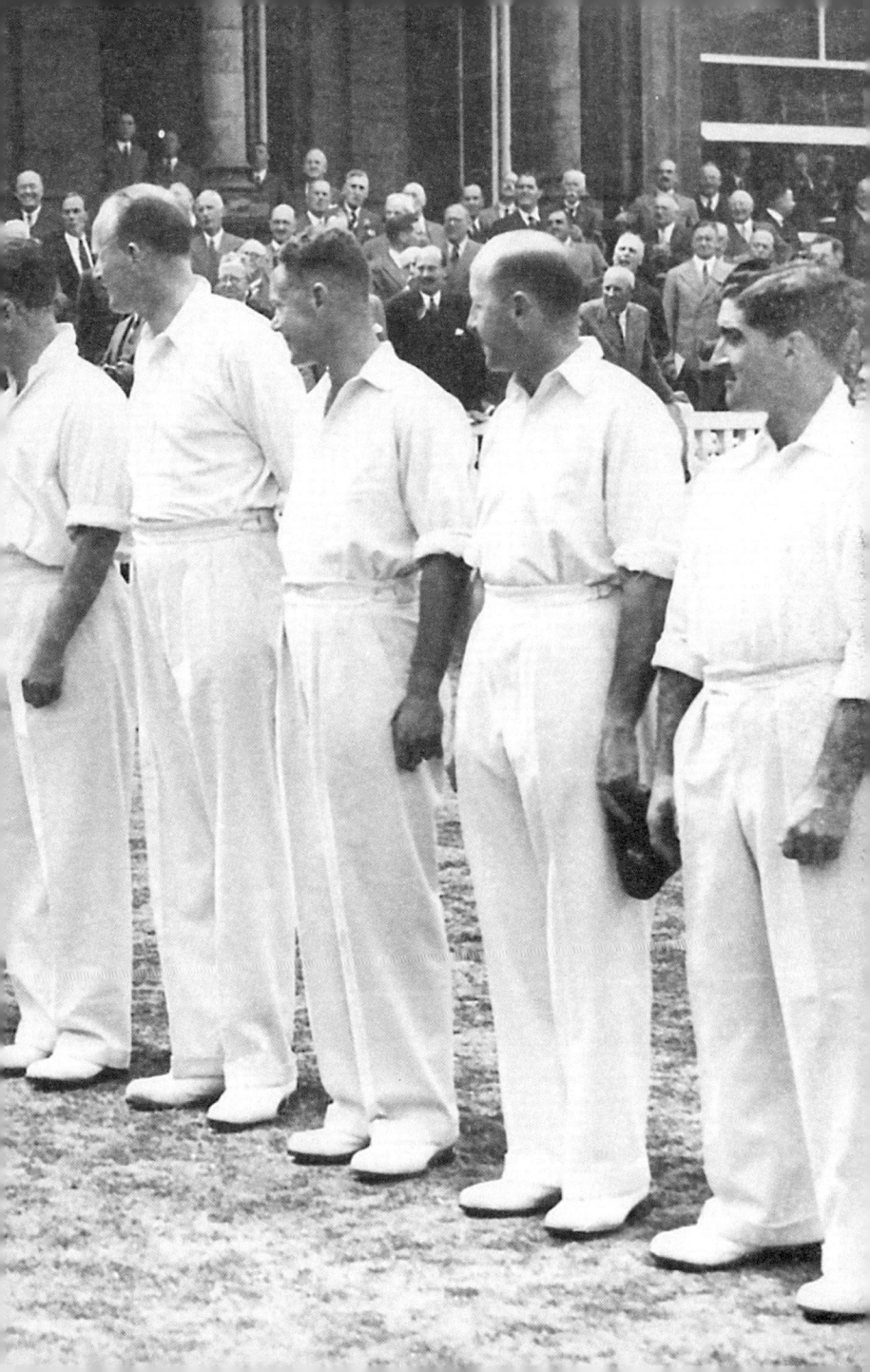

with Bradman undefeated on 173 as Australia scored the winning runs. Bradman's duck (after needing just 4 to secure a Test average of 100) was Australia's only lowlight of an innings and 149 run win at The Oval. England were bowled out for 52 in its first innings, with Lindwall's 6 for 20 doing the damage. Morris was run out on 196 in Australia's only innings of 389.

NEWSPAPER HEADLINE

Invincibles Retain Ashes for Australia

THE SCOREBOARD

FIRST TEST: 10–15 June (Trent Bridge)
Australia won by 8 wickets
England 165 and 441
Australia 509 and 2 for 98

SECOND TEST: 24–29 June (Lord's)
Australia won by 409 runs
Australia 350 and 7 dec. for 460
England 215 and 186

THIRD TEST: 8–13 July (Old Trafford)
Match Drawn
England 363 and 3 dec. for 174
Australia 221 and 1 for 92

FOURTH TEST: 22–27 July (Headingley)
Australia won by 7 wickets
England 496 and 8 dec. for 365
Australia 458 and 3 for 404

FIFTH TEST: 14–18 August (The Oval)
Australia won by an innings and 149 runs
England 52 and 188
Australia 389

FACEBOOK MOMENT

England failed to make inroads into Australia's batting in the second innings at Leeds in the Fourth Test, where Australia chased down 404 runs with 10 minutes to spare in 334 minutes.

FOR THE RECORD

Most Runs:	AR Morris (AUS) 696
Most Wickets:	RR Lindwall (AUS), WA Johnston (AUS) 27
Highest Score:	AR Morris (AUS) 196 (Fifth Test)
Best Bowling:	RR Lindwall (AUS) 6 for 20 (Fifth Test)
Most Catches:	KR Miller (AUS) 8
Highest Run	AR Morris/DG Bradman (AUS) 301
Partnership:	(Fourth Test, 2nd wicket)

Centuries:

England	Australia
DS Compton (2)	SG Barnes
WJ Edrich	DG Bradman (2)
C Washbrook	RN Harvey
	AL Hassett
	AR Morris (3)

TWITTER FACT

Sid Barnes spent 10 days in hospital after being hit under the ribs fielding at short leg in the Third Test at Old Trafford.

DID YOU KNOW?

At the time of writing, Neil Harvey – aged 88 – is the last remaining 'Invincible'.

CHAPTER 7

THE 1950s

FRANK TYSON, ENGLAND

1950–51
IN AUSTRALIA

AUSTRALIA	V	ENGLAND
AL HASSETT		FR BROWN
WON	DRAWN	WON
4	0	1

Freddie Brown was the third choice as England captain and led a young and inexperienced side to Australia for the 1950–51 Ashes. It was still hoped England would make amends for their thrashing in the previous series. At Brisbane, the home side failed to capitalise on a good batting surface scoring 228 with Neil Harvey top scoring with 74. Rain interrupted and England declared at 7 for 68 wanting to make the most of the sticky wicket. Bill Johnston with 5 for 35, the key destroyer. Australia was 3 for 0 in the second innings with Jack Moroney's only Ashes Test ending in a pair. Hassett closed Australia's second innings at 7 for 32. Despite Hutton's undefeated 62 England was bowled out for 122, still 71 runs in arrears. Melbourne's low scoring match saw England lead by three runs on the first innings. England's Brian Close aged 19 played his only Test of the series scoring 0 and 1. Australia's new 'mystery' bowler Jack Iverson took six wickets as Australia won by 28 runs. In Sydney, Keith Miller's unconquered 145 was the highlight in Australia's 426 which proved too much for England. Iverson was the match winner for Australia, taking 6 for 26. Morris scored a double century out of Australia's first innings 371 at Adelaide. Len Hutton managed 57 percent of England's 272 with 156 not out. Burke at the age of 20 scored a ton in his debut Test as Australia careered ahead with 8 declared for 403. Brown who had been injured in a car accident was unable to bat in his side's second innings, which managed only 228. Reg Simpson's undefeated 156 set England up to win the final Test at the MCG after Australia was bowled out for 217. Alec Bedser's five second innings wickets (after five in the first) helped bowl Australia out for 197.

NEWSPAPER HEADLINE

Easy Ashes Win for Australia

THE SCOREBOARD

FIRST TEST: 1–5 December (Brisbane)
Australia won by 70 runs
Australia 228 and 7 dec. for 32
England 7 dec. for 68 and 122

SECOND TEST: 22–27 December (Melbourne)
Australia won by 28 runs
Australia 194 and 181
England 197 and 150

THIRD TEST: 6 January – 9 January (Sydney)
Australia won by an innings and 13 runs
Australia 290 and 123
England 426

FOURTH TEST: 2–8 February (Adelaide)
Australia won by 274 runs
Australia 371 and 8 dec. for 403
England 272 and 228

FIFTH TEST: 23–28 February (Melbourne)
England won by 8 wickets
Australia 217 and 197
England 320 and 2 for 95.

FACEBOOK MOMENT

When Australia's Jack Iverson, who bowled with a 'bent finger grip and mystified the England batsmen', took 6 for 27 routing the England team for 123 in its second innings, Australia had retained the Ashes.

FOR THE RECORD

Most Runs:	L Hutton (ENG) 533
Most Wickets:	AV Bedser (ENG) 30
Highest Score:	AR Morris (AUS) 206 (Fourth Test)
Best Bowling:	JB Iverson (AUS) 6 for 27 (Third Test)
Most Catches:	L Hutton (ENG) 9
Highest Run Partnership:	KR Miller/IWG Johnson (AUS) 150 (Third Test, 7th wicket)

Centuries:

England	**Australia**
L Hutton	JW Burke
RT Simpson	KR Miller
	AR Morris

TWITTER FACT

England's star batsman Denis Compton averaged just 7 for the series while Len Hutton averaged 88.

DID YOU KNOW?

The Second Test at the MCG included a two-day rest for Sunday and Christmas Day.

1953
IN ENGLAND

ENGLAND	V	AUSTRALIA
L HUTTON		AL HASSETT
WON	DRAWN	WON
1	4	0

England won its first home Ashes series for 27 years, (despite the Australian captain Lindsay Hassett calling correctly at the toss in all five Test matches). Hutton became the first professional to captain England at home during the First Test at Trent Bridge, where Alec Bedser's 14 wickets for the match meant Australia struggled at one stage losing its last seven wickets for 12 runs.

Hassett's first innings 115 was the stand out for Australia. Hassett scored a second consecutive ton as he opened in the place of Graeme Hole (who had failed twice in the first encounter) as Australia reached 346. Hutton's brilliant 145 helped England to a 26 run lead. A Keith Miller century helped set England 343 to win but Willie Watson's defensive 109 combined with Trevor Bailey's 71 in more than four hours saved the day. Rain wiped out all but 13 hours of play in the Third Test at Old Trafford where Johnny Wardle's wrist spinners took seven wickets for the match including 4 for 7 in Australia's second innings as they collapsed to 8 for 35. Australia led by 99 after sending England in to bat at Headingley. Bailey again batted for more than 4 hours, this time scoring just 38. Australia's chase for 177 ended at 4 for 147 when Bailey saved the game by bowling down the leg side. With the series locked at nil–all, the Fifth Test at the Oval was extended to six days. Fred Trueman, brought in for his first Test of the summer, took 4 first innings wickets as Australia stumbled to 275. Hutton made 82 as England locked in a lead of 31. Jim Laker and Tony Lock combined to take 9 Australian wickets in a second innings collapse, that saw them bowled out for 162. England scored the necessary runs for the loss of two wickets and the Ashes returned to England for the first time in almost 19 years.

NEWSPAPER HEADLINE

England, at Last!

THE SCOREBOARD

FIRST TEST: 11–16 June (Trent Bridge)
Match Drawn
Australia 249 and 123
England 144 and 1 for 120

SECOND TEST: 25–30 June (Lord's)
Match Drawn
Australia 346 and 368
England 372 and 7 for 282

THIRD TEST: 9–14 July (Old Trafford)
Match Drawn
Australia 318 and 8 for 35
England 276

FOURTH TEST: 22–28 July (Headingley)
Match Drawn
England 167 and 275
Australia 266 and 4 for 147

FIFTH TEST: 15–19 August (The Oval)
England won by 8 wickets
Australia 275 and 162
England 306 and 2 for 132.

FACEBOOK MOMENT

In the decider at The Oval, Laker and Lock reduced Australia to 6 for 86 (after being 1 for 59). Ken Archer and Alan Davidson added 50 trying to hit their way out of trouble but it was to no avail. Australia lost by eight wickets.

FOR THE RECORD

Most Runs:	L Hutton (ENG) 443	
Most Wickets:	AV Bedser (ENG) 39	
Highest Score:	L Hutton 145 (Second Test)	
Best Bowling:	AV Bedser (ENG) 7 for 44 (First Test)	
Most Catches:	GB Hole (AUS) 8	
Highest Run	RN Harvey/GB Hole (AUS) 173	
Partnership:	(Third Test, 4th wicket)	
Centuries:	**England**	**Australia**
	L Hutton	AL Hassett (2)
	W Watson	RN Harvey
		KR Miller

TWITTER FACT

England's Chairman of selectors Freddie Brown came out of retirement for the Second Test, taking four second innings wickets.

DID YOU KNOW?

Australia's fast bowler Bill Johnston, led the first-class batting averages, being dismissed only once on tour while accumulating 102 runs.

1954–55
IN AUSTRALIA

AUSTRALIA	v	ENGLAND
IW JOHNSTON (1, 3–5) AR MORRIS (2)		L HUTTON
WON	DRAWN	WON
1	1	3

Complete covering of the pitch didn't stop Len Hutton from sending
Australia in to bat on a lively surface in Brisbane. The tactic failed
as Australia mounted a formidable 8 declared for 601. Morris (153)
and Harvey (162) added 202 in a little more than four hours. Not
even the plodder Trevor Bailey (88 and 23) could stop England being
dismissed twice and still be 153 runs in arrears. England's Frank
Tyson had figures of 1 for 160 from 29 overs, the calm before the
storm. Morris filling in for injured skipper Ian Johnson, put England
into bat knocking them over for 154. Australia replied with 228 with
Ron Archer's 49 the top score of the match to date. The home side took
the upper hand as England fell to 3 for 55, when a Peter May (104)
and Colin Cowdrey stand of 116 set the Australians 223. Tyson still
reeling from being knocked out by a Lindwall bouncer returned fire
taking his 10th wicket for the match and bowling Australia out for
184. Neil Harvey's undefeated 92, the only sign of defiance. 63,814
Melbourne fans witnessed a fine Colin Cowdrey century, as Miller
and Archer snared seven wickets between them, bowled England out
for 191. Brian Statham ripped through Australia's batting line-up as
keeper Len Maddocks top scored with 47 out of 231. May's 91 enabled
England to get to 279. Australia chasing 240 were annihilated as
Tyson took 7 for 27 second innings wickets with the last 8 wickets
falling for 34 runs. Controversy surrounded the match, when it was
revealed the groundsman had watered the pitch on the rest day
after hot weather opened up cracks in preceding days. At Adelaide's

Australia scored 323, with Len Maddocks leading the way with 69. England crawled past with 341, with Hutton (80) and Colin Cowdrey (79) proving resourceful. Australia collapsed again, *The Advertiser* reporting, 'a lame and impotent display of batting,' dismissed for 111. Despite losing three early wickets England chased down the small total, with five wickets remaining. England's victory in a rain-affected Fifth Test sealed their first Ashes series win in Australia since 'Bodyline' in 1932–33.

NEWSPAPER HEADLINE

England Bring Ashes Home

THE SCOREBOARD

FIRST TEST: 26 November–1 December (Brisbane)
Australia won by an innings and 154 runs
Australia 601
England 190 and 257

SECOND TEST: 17–22 December (Sydney)
England won by 38 runs
England 154 and 296
Australia 228 and 184

THIRD TEST: 1 December–5 January (Melbourne)
England 191 and 279
Australia 231 and 111
England won by 128 runs

FOURTH TEST: 28 January–2 February (Adelaide)
Match Drawn
England 7 dec. for 371
Australia 221 and 6 for 118

FIFTH TEST: 25 February–3 March (Sydney)
England won by 5 wickets
Australia 323 and 111
England 341 and 5 for 97

FACEBOOK MOMENT

When Australia was bowled out for 111 in its second innings of the Third Test at Melbourne. Tyson's 6 for 16 in 51 balls to help route Australia.

FOR THE RECORD

Most Runs:	RN Harvey (AUS) 354
Most Wickets:	FH Tyson (ENG) 28
Highest Score:	RN Harvey (AUS) 162 (First Test)
Best Bowling:	FH Tyson (ENG) 7 for 27 (Third Test)
Most Catches:	PBH May (ENG) 6
Highest Run Partnership:	AR Morris/RN Harvey (AUS) 202 (First Test, 3rd wicket)

Centuries:

England	**Australia**
PBH May	RN Harvey
MC Cowdrey	
AR Morris	
TW Graveney	

TWITTER FACT

England bowled Australia out twice for the unlucky score of 111 during the series.

DID YOU KNOW?

This was England Colin Cowdrey's first of six tours of England that would stretch until 1974–75.

1956
IN ENGLAND

ENGLAND	V	AUSTRALIA
PBH MAY		IW JOHNSON
WON	DRAWN	WON
2	2	1

Continual wet weather and the off-spinning skills of Jim Laker proved too much for an Australian side led by Ian Johnson. In the rain interrupted opening Test of the series (12 hours were lost) at Trent Bridge, not even two declarations could force a result. The biggest blow for Australia was when Alan Davidson had to be carried off the field because of a chipped ankle. Australia triumphed at Lord's with Keith Miller taking ten wickets for the match and wicketkeeper Gil Langley, creating a Test record with nine victims. England selector Cyril Washbrook was brought back into the side at the age of 41 after an absence of five years at Headingley. The veteran proved his worth scoring 98, adding 187 with skipper Peter May after England were teetering at 3 for 17. Laker took 11 wickets for the match as Australia was bowled out twice for 143 and 140. Neil Harvey scored 69 in the second innings in Australia's first defeat at Leeds. In what would become known as 'Lakers Match', the England off spinner took 19 wickets for the match, all from the Stretford End at Old Trafford. England's first innings 459 included centuries from opener Peter Richardson and The Reverend David Shepherd. Neil Harvey scored two ducks on the second day as Australia, battling a now dusty pitch, was dismissed for 84 with Laker taking 9 for 37 (including 7 for 8 in 22 balls). The third and fourth days were storm interrupted, while on the fifth Laker finished with 10 for 53. Colin McDonald's gritty 89 had lasted 337 minutes. More than 12 hours were also lost during the drawn Fifth Test at The Oval. A recalled Denis Compton scored 94 to help England lead on the first innings. A second innings declaration from the home side made no difference as Australia completed the Test series at 5 for 27. Laker's seven wickets took his haul to 46 wickets for the series, an Ashes record.

NEWSPAPER HEADLINE

Laker's Ashes!

THE SCOREBOARD

FIRST TEST: 7–12 June (Trent Bridge)
Match Drawn
England 217 and 3 for 188
Australia 148 and 3 for 120

SECOND TEST: 21–26 June (Lord's)
Australia won by 185 runs
Australia 285 and 257
England 171 and 186

THIRD TEST: 12–17 July (Headingley)
England won by an innings and 42 runs
England 325
Australia 143 and 140

FOURTH TEST: 26–31 July (Old Trafford)
England won by an innings and 170 runs
England 459
Australia 84 and 205

FIFTH TEST: 23–28 August (The Oval)
Match Drawn
England 247 and 3 dec. for 182
202 and 5 for 27

FACEBOOK MOMENT

Jim Laker's spell of 7 for 8 in 22 balls to help bowl Australia out for 84 in its first innings at Old Trafford. He followed up his nine first innings wickets with ten in the second.

FOR THE RECORD

Most Runs:	PBH May (ENG) 453
Most Wickets:	JC Laker (ENG) 46
Highest Score:	Rev DS Sheppard (ENG) 113 (Fourth Test)
Best Bowling:	Jim Laker (ENG) 10 for 53 (Fourth Test)
	* Ashes record
Most Catches:	GAR Lock (ENG) 10
Highest Run	PBH May/C Washbrook (ENG) 187
Partnership:	(Third Test, 4th wicket)
Centuries:	**England**
	PBH May
	PE Richardson
	Rev DS Sheppard

TWITTER FACT

On a pitch favouring spin at Old Trafford, England's left-arm orthodox spinner Tony Lock took only one wicket.

DID YOU KNOW?

After the Old Trafford Test Jim Laker stopped off at a pub in Lichfield on the way to London to play for Surrey to grab a beer and a sandwich. He sat unrecognised in the crowded pub as people around him watched the highlights on television.

1958–59
IN AUSTRALIA

AUSTRALIA	v	ENGLAND
R BENAUD		PBH MAY
WON	DRAWN	WON
4	1	0

The 1958–59 Ashes was the first to be televised live into Australian
homes, as it featured some of the slowest scoring ever. Australia won
at the Gabba by eight wickets. England's Trevor Bailey's batted for
458 minutes for 68 in his side's second innings while Australia's Jim
Burke made an undefeated 28 in more than four hours. It was one
of the lowest points in Ashes cricket. Alan Davidson's second over in
Melbourne took three vital wickets (Peter Richardson, Willie Watson
and Tom Graveney) although England recovered with the help of a
century from captain Peter May (the first by an England captain in
Australia for 56 years). Neil Harvey's 167 helped Australia lead by 49.
England opening bowler Brian Statham took 7 for 57. Ian Meckiff's six
second innings wickets rolled the visitors for 87, as Australia repeated
its victory margin of the First Test. Richie Benaud's five wickets gave
Australia the upper hand when England was bowled out for 219. Colin
Cowdrey's second innings century meant Australia had to chase 150
runs in just under two hours; they finished at 2 for 54. Australia's
dominance continued at Adelaide where a Colin McDonald's 170 saw
Australia's first innings 476 overwhelm England. Benaud's nine match
wickets added to his haul at Sydney. Trevor Bailey ended his Ashes
career with a pair in the final Test at the MCG as England tumbled
to be all out for 205 and 214. McDonald made his second successive
century as Australia coasted to a nine-wicket win. Some bitterness
over the bowling actions of Australia bowlers Ian Meckiff, Keith
Slater, Gordon Rorke and Jim Burke remained after the series ended.

RICHIE BENAUD, AUSTRALIA

NEWSPAPER HEADLINE

Benaud Leads Australia to Ashes Victory!

THE SCOREBOARD

FIRST TEST: 5–10 December (Brisbane)
Australia won by 8 wickets
England 134 and 198
Australia 186 and 2 for 147

SECOND TEST: 31 December–5 January (Melbourne)
Australia won by 8 wickets
England 259 and 87
Australia 308 and 2 for 42

THIRD TEST: 9–15 January (Sydney)
Match Drawn
England 219 and 7 dec. for 287
Australia 357 and 2 for 54

FOURTH TEST: 30 January–5 February (Adelaide)
Australia won by 10 wickets
Australia 476 and 0 for 36
England 240 and 270

FIFTH TEST: 13–18 February (Melbourne)
Australia won by 9 wickets
England 205 and 214
Australia 251 and 1 for 69.

FACEBOOK MOMENT

Australia captain Richie Benaud's consecutive nine wicket hauls at Adelaide saw the home side regain the Ashes with a ten wicket win.

FOR THE RECORD

Most Runs:	CC McDonald (AUS) 520
Most Wickets:	R Benaud (AUS) 31
Highest Score:	CC McDonald (AUS) 170 (Fourth Test)
Best Bowling:	JB Statham (ENG) 7 for 57 (Second Test)
Most Catches:	R Benaud (AUS) 8
Highest Run	PBH May/MC Cowdrey (ENG) 182
Partnership:	(Third Test, 4th wicket)

Centuries:

England	**Australia**
MC Cowdrey	RN Harvey
PBH May	CC McDonald (2)

TWITTER FACT

England's second innings score of 87 at Melbourne was its lowest total in Australia since 1903–04.

DID YOU KNOW?

Australia's nemesis in 1956 off spinner Jim Laker wasn't the same bowler on hard and fast Australian pitches and finished with only 15 Test wickets for the tour.

CHAPTER 8

THE 1960s

BOB SIMPSON, AUSTRALIA

1961 IN ENGLAND

ENGLAND	v	AUSTRALIA
MC COWDREY (1–2)		R BENAUD (1, 3–5)
PBH MAY (3–5)		RN HARVEY (2)
WON	DRAWN	WON
1	2	2

It was the most enthralling Test series of recent times. By 1961 bowlers whose actions were considered suspicious were not selected for either side. Ken Mackay's three wickets in four balls (Ken Barrington, Raman Subba Row and Mike Smith) provided the Australian highlight as England collapsed to be all out for 195 in the first innings at Edgbaston. Neil Harvey registered his 20th Test match hundred as Australia responded strongly with 9 declared for 516. Raman Subba Row (in his first Ashes Test) and Ted Dexter scored second innings tons as the match ended in a draw. Harvey replaced Richie Benaud (shoulder injury) as captain at Lord's where Alan Davidson took 5 for 42 as England were dismissed for 206. Bill Lawry playing in just his second Test, batted for 367 minutes scoring 130. Graham McKenzie on debut took five English second innings wickets while Australia lost five wickets chasing 71 needed for victory. May and Benaud returned as captains when England won at Leeds. Fred Trueman's 11 wickets for the match included 6 for 30 in Australia's 120. (including Benaud for a pair). Cowdrey's 93 the high-water mark for batsmen during the match. The Fourth Test at Old Trafford is often cited as one of the best comebacks in Ashes history. Bill Lawry was Australia's highest scorer with 74 out of 190. Brian Statham's 5 for 53, the main destroyer. The match again tilted England's way as Peter May scored 95 out of 367. Australia responded with 432 Lawry again excelling scoring 102. Alan Davidson's undefeated 77, put on 98 with McKenzie, including 20 off one over from off spinner David Allen. Benaud famously bowled his side to a win, taking 5 for 12 in 25 deliveries, aiming at the rough coming around the wicket. Dexter shone striking 76 but it wasn't enough. Australia had won the Test by

54 runs and retained the Ashes. Third and fourth day rain at the Fifth Test at The Oval saw a drawn match. Norm O'Neill and Peter Burge made their first hundreds against England while Lawry experienced a rare failure (out for a duck) in Australia's first innings of 494. Subba Row scored 137 (98 with a runner after injuring his leg) while Mackay took five second innings wickets.

NEWSPAPER HEADLINE

Benaud's Aussies Retain Ashes

THE SCOREBOARD

FIRST TEST: 8–13 June (Edgbaston)
Match Drawn
England 195 and 4 for 401
Australia 9 dec. for 516

SECOND TEST: 22–26 June (Lord's)
Australia won by 5 wickets
England 206 and 202
Australia 340 and 5 for 71

THIRD TEST: 6–8 July (Headingley)
England won by 8 wickets
Australia 237 and 120
England 299 and 2 for 62

FOURTH TEST: 27 July–1 August (Old Trafford)
Australia won by 54 runs
Australia 190 and 432
England 367 and 201

FIFTH TEST: 17–22 August (The Oval)
Match Drawn
England 256 and 8 for 370
Australia 494

FACEBOOK MOMENT

The Australian captain's dynamic spell of leg spin bowling helped reduce England from 1 for 150 to all out 201 in the Fourth Test at Old Trafford. His 6 for 70 off 32 overs bowling around the wicket and into the rough retained the Ashes for Australia.

FOR THE RECORD

Most Runs:	WM Lawry (AUS) 420
Most Wickets:	AK Davidson (AUS) 23
Highest Score:	PJP Burge (AUS) 181 (Fifth Test)
Best Bowling:	FS Trueman (ENG) 6 for 30 (Third Test)
Most Catches:	RB Simpson (AUS) 7
Highest Run Partnership:	PJP Burge/BC Booth (AUS) 185 (Fifth Test, 5th wicket)

Centuries:

England	**Australia**
ER Dexter	PJP Burge
R Subba Row (2)	RN Harvey
	WM Lawry (2)
	NCL O'Neill

TWITTER FACT

England's Raman Subba Row scored centuries in his first and last Ashes Tests (all in the same series).

DID YOU KNOW?

Wicketkeepers for both sides had a terrific series. Australia's Wally Grout set a new Ashes record with 21 victims while England's John Murray managed 18, a new England record for a home series.

1962–63
IN AUSTRALIA

AUSTRALIA	V	ENGLAND
R BENAUD		ER DEXTER
WON	DRAWN	WON
1	3	1

A series that did not live up to its potential while the Australian authorities introduced a scheduling of six hours per day for the first time. The drawn Brisbane opener saw 14 fifties scored in the match, with just one century, by Australia's Brian Booth (112). England's captain Ted Dexter made 99 as his side finished the final day at 6 for 278 in pursuit of 378. Seven bowlers were tried by each of the sides at Melbourne. Another Colin Cowdrey ton at the MCG meant England led by 15 on the first innings. Lawry's second half century of the match in more than four hours and Booth's 103 saved the Australian side from embarrassment. The Reverend David Sheppard's second innings 113, the England highlight as they chased down the required runs with seven wickets in hand. Australia's wicketkeeper Barry Jarman took one of the most sensational catches seen at the MCG when he caught Geoff Pullar down the leg side for 5. Part-time leg spinner and opening batsman Bob Simpson's five wicket haul at Sydney reduced England to 279 in its first innings. Simpson then backed up with 91 while Test debutante Barry Shepherd scored an impressive undefeated 71. Fred Titmus' (7 for 79) wily off spinners bowled Australia out for 319. Davidson's five wicket second innings haul brought his total to nine for the match as England succumbed for 104. Injured England wicketkeeper John Murray batted 100 minutes for his undefeated 3. After the early losses of Lawry and Harvey, Australia swept to victory by eight wickets and levelled the series. Adelaide was a high scoring affair as Harvey and Norm O'Neill scored centuries in a first innings of 393. Ken Barrington's 132 not out in England's second innings (where he struck a six to reach his hundred) was England's main highlight of the drawn match. Barrington's second consecutive Test ton set England up for a solid first innings. In Sydney Titmus was again in the wickets with 5 for 103 off 47 overs. Australia started out in its chase of 241 runs in 240 minutes with two early wickets, before finishing lamely at 4 for 152. The drawn match marked the end of the careers of Alan Davidson and Neil Harvey.

NEWSPAPER HEADLINE

Drawn Rubber: Aussies retain Ashes

THE SCOREBOARD

FIRST TEST: 1–5 December (Brisbane)
Match Drawn
Australia 404 and 4 dec. for 362
England 389 and 6 for 278

SECOND TEST: 29 December–3 January (Melbourne)
England won by 7 wickets
Australia 316 and 248
England 331 and 3 for 237

THIRD TEST: 11–15 January (Sydney)
Australia won by 8 wickets
England 279 and 104
Australia 319 and 2 for 67

FOURTH TEST: 25–30 January (Adelaide)
Match Drawn
Australia 393 and 293
England 331 and 4 for 223

FIFTH TEST: 15–20 February (Sydney)
Match Drawn
England 321 and 8 dec. for 268
Australia 349 and 4 for 152

FACEBOOK MOMENT

Australia chose to play out time rather than chase the runs on the final day of the Fifth Test. Alan Davidson took a wicket with his last ball in Test Cricket, having Alan Smith caught at first slip by Bobby Simpson.

FOR THE RECORD

Most Runs: KF Barrington (ENG) 502
Most Wickets: AK Davidson (AUS) 24
Highest Score: RN Harvey (AUS) 154 (Fourth Test)
Best Bowling: FJ Titmus (ENG) 7 for 79 (Third Test)
Most Catches: R Benaud (AUS) 9
Highest Run   RN Harvey/NCL O'Neill (AUS) 194
Partnership: (Fourth Test, 4th wicket)
Centuries:

England	Australia
KF Barrington (2)	BC Booth (2)
MC Cowdrey	PJP Burge
Rev DS Sheppard	RN Harvey
	WM Lawry
	NCL O'Neill

TWITTER FACT

The 1962–63 summer produced the first drawn Ashes series in Australia.

DID YOU KNOW?

At Adelaide, England's middle order batsman Ken Barrington struck a six to bring up his ton, becoming just the second batsman after Australia's Joe Darling (1897/98) to do so.

1964
IN ENGLAND

ENGLAND	v	AUSTRALIA
ER DEXTER		RB SIMPSON
WON	DRAWN	WON
0	4	1

Rain again intervened with much of the 1964 Ashes series. More than 14 hours was lost in the First Test at Trent Bridge. Geoffrey Boycott began his Ashes career with 48. Graham McKenzie's second innings 5 for 53 provided an Australian highlight in the drawn match. Australia's rain interrupted chase for 242 in 195 minutes only lasted 45 minutes but not before O'Neill had hooked Fred Trueman for boundaries from the first four balls of his second over. Play was washed out for the first two days of the much-anticipated Lord's Test on the ground's 150th anniversary. Trueman's five first innings wickets bowled Australia out for 176. John Edrich's first innings hundred (120) in his inaugural Ashes Test, the high score of England's 246. Edrich's consumption of 317 minutes and Australia's slow second innings, including Ian Redpath's three and a ¼ hour 36, ensured a draw when the rain came once more. Australia won the only result of the series at Headingly by seven wickets. Neil Hawke's medium pacers took five England wickets in their first innings 268. Peter Burge's 160, helped take the Australian total from 7 for 178 to 389 (Wally Grout and Hawke both scored 37). Titmus opened the bowling in Australia's second innings (Jack Flavell) as they chased down 111 runs with seven wickets in hand. Ian Redpath, 58 not out, hit the winning runs. At Old Trafford, Australian captain Bob Simpson's first innings 311, over more than two days was his first Test century. After Lawry (106) and Simpson added 201 they scored 656. Ken Barrington's 256 and Ted Dexter's 174 proved how much of a featherbed the pitch was. McKenzie took seven second innings wickets while Tom Veivers 95 overs. Another draw at The Oval after Fred Trueman became the first bowler to take 300 Test wickets.

NEWSPAPER HEADLINE

Australia Again in Rain-Interrupted Series

THE SCOREBOARD

FIRST TEST: 4–9 June (Trent Bridge)
Match Drawn
England 216 and 9 dec. for 193
Australia 168 and 2 for 40

SECOND TEST: 18–23 June (Lord's)
Match Drawn
Australia 176 and 4 for 168
England 246

THIRD TEST: 2–6 July (Headingley)
Australia won by 7 wickets
England 268 and 229
Australia 389 and 3 for 111

FOURTH TEST: 23–28 July (Old Trafford)
Match Drawn
Australia 656 and 0 for 4
England 611

FIFTH TEST: 13–18 August (The Oval)
Match Drawn
England 182 and 4 for 381
Australia 379

FACEBOOK MOMENT

Australia's Peter Burge scored 160, helping Australia to 389 after being 7 for 178 in its first innings. England were bowled out for 229 in its second innings meaning a low run chase for the home side.

FOR THE RECORD

Most Runs: RB Simpson (AUS) 458
Most Wickets: GD McKenzie (AUS) 29
Highest Score: RB Simpson (AUS) 311 (Fourth Test)
Best Bowling: GD McKenzie (AUS) 7 for 153 (Fourth Test)
Most Catches: RB Simpson (AUS) 8
Highest Run   ER Dexter/KF Barrington (ENG) 246
Partnership: (Fourth Test, 3rd wicket)
Centuries: **England**   **Australia**
                         KF Barrington   PJP Burge
                         G Boycott   WM Lawry
                         ER Dexter   RB Simpson
                         JH Edrich

TWITTER FACT

The 1964 Australia side was the first to fly to England rather than travel by ship.

DID YOU KNOW?

Australian captain Bob Simpson had to wait until his 30th Test, and his 51st innings, to score a century. He batted almost 13 hours for his 311, the highest Test innings scored at Old Trafford.

1965–66
IN AUSTRALIA

AUSTRALIA	v	ENGLAND
BC BOOTH (1, 3) RB SIMPSON (2, 4, 5)		MJ SMITH
WON	DRAWN	WON
1	3	1

The drawn Ashes series continued in Australia in 1965/66. Brian Booth captained Australia at a rain interrupted encounter at Brisbane (Simpson had a fractured wrist). Nineteen-year-old Doug Walters began his Test career with 155 as Australia waltzed to 443, also aided by Bill Lawry's 166. Leg spinner Peter Philpott took five wickets in England's first innings 280 with Fred Titmus (60) top scoring. England followed-on to be 3 for 186 by the time the match petered out to a draw. Returning captain Simpson made two half centuries in Melbourne as his side made 358 and 426. Walters scored his second hundred of the series (making it two hundreds in his first two Tests) as Burge atoned for his First Test duck with 115. Cowdrey managed his third ton at the MCG as England answered with 558 in the drawn match. McKenzie toiled well to take 5 for 134 from 35 overs. England continued its high scoring with 448 in its first innings at Sydney. England's flamboyant left hand opening batsman Bob Barber notched his only Test century making it a big one (185) while John Edrich's second ton came in successive innings. Neil Hawke's 7 for 105 was the only home bowler to have much effect. Australia again without Simpson (chickenpox) fell short in both innings as spinners Fred Titmus and David Allen, took eight wickets between them in the second innings. Adelaide saw Australia mount a formidable total with Simpson and Lawry adding 244 for the first wicket. Simpson's nine hour, 225–run response to England's first innings 241 (with McKenzie's 6 for 48 doing the most damage). A second innings hundred by Ken Barrington couldn't stop the rot with Hawke taking his second five wicket haul for the series. Barrington made it two tons on the trot in the Fifth Test at the MCG, again reaching a hundred with a six. Bob Cowper's 307 in twelve hours meant that the only result could be a draw.

NEWSPAPER HEADLINE

Australia's Ashes After Drawn Series

THE SCOREBOARD

FIRST TEST: 10–15 December (Brisbane)
Match Drawn
Australia 6 dec. for 443
England 280 and 3 for 186

SECOND TEST: 30 December–4 January (Melbourne)
Match Drawn
Australia 358 and 426
England 558

THIRD TEST: 7–11 January (Sydney)
England won by innings and 93 runs
England 488
Australia 221 and 174

FOURTH TEST: 28 January–1 February (Adelaide Oval)
Australia won by an innings and nine runs
England 241 and 166
Australia 516

FIFTH TEST: 11–16 February (Melbourne)
Match Drawn
England 485 and 3 for 69
Australia 543

FACEBOOK MOMENT

Bob Cowper's 307 in the final Test at Melbourne, consumed 727 minutes, the longest first-class innings in Australia, ending any chance of a result other than a stalemate.

FOR THE RECORD

Most Runs:	WM Lawry (AUS) 592
Most Wickets:	NJN Hawke (AUS), GD McKenzie (AUS) 16
Highest Score:	RM Cowper (AUS) 307 (Fifth Test)
Best Bowling:	NJN Hawke (AUS) 7 for 105 (Third Test)
Most Catches:	MC Cowdrey (ENG) 4
Highest Run	RB Simpson/WM Lawry (AUS) 244
Partnership:	(Fourth Test, 1st wicket)

Centuries:

England	Australia
RW Barber	PJP Burge
K Barrington (2)	RM Cowper
MC Cowdrey	WM Lawry (3)
JH Edrich (2)	RB Simpson
	KD Walters (2)

TWITTER FACT

When Doug Walters (aged 19 years 357 days) scored a century in his first Test, he was Australia's third youngest behind Neil Harvey and Archie Jackson in an Ashes Test.

DID YOU KNOW?

Australia's wicketkeeper Wally Grout ended his stellar career with 187 dismissals from 51 Tests. Debuting against South Africa in 1957/58 at the age of 30, Grout proved one of Australia's most reliable stumpers. Sadly, two years after he retired, he died of a heart attack at the age of 41.

1968
IN ENGLAND

ENGLAND	v	AUSTRALIA
WM LAWRY (1–3, 5)		MC COWDREY (1–3, 5)
BN JARMAN (4)		TW GRAVENEY (4)

WON	DRAWN	WON
1	3	1

The 1968 Ashes provided the fourth drawn rubber of the decade as rain again spoiled playing opportunities. Australia started the series at Old Trafford with a respectable 357 with Doug Walters (81), Paul Sheahan (88) and Ian Chappell (73) all scoring half centuries in their England debuts. Bob Cowper's gentle off spinners took four wickets as England fell for 165. Pat Pocock's more troublesome spinners captured 6 for 79 in as Australia was reduced to a second innings 220. Walters produced 86 in what would be his most productive Test match of his four England tours. As Dennis Amiss fell for a pair in his Ashes debut, South African-born Basil D'Oliveira batted defiantly for an undefeated 87 as England lost the First Test by 159 runs. England's strongest performers in the First Test, (Pocock and D'Oliveira) were dropped for the Second Test at Lord's which lost more than half of its playing hours through rain. England bowled the visitors out for 78 after scoring 351 including Colin Milburn's explosive innings of 83 and David Brown's swing bowling taking 5 for 42. The much celebrated 200th match between the rivals ended in a draw as Australia finished at 4 for 127. Colin Cowdrey celebrated his 100th Test match with 104 in England's first innings 409 at Edgbaston while Tom Graveney fell four short of the milestone. Ian Chappell's 76, the main leading light as Australia was again shot out, this time for 222 (Bill Lawry retired hurt having fractured a finger). Headingley provided another

BASIL D'OLIVEIRA AND TOM GRAVENEY, ENGLAND

draw as Tom Graveney and Barry Jarman filled in for their respective captains. Ian Redpath's first innings 92, the highest score for the match. Australia and England both played defensively as England chasing 326 ending at 4 for 230. England won the Fifth Test with just minutes to spare when Derek Underwood (7 for 50) bowled Australia out for 125. Ground staff worked overtime to 'mop up' the wet ground after long periods of rain.

NEWSPAPER HEADLINE

The Oval 'Mop Up' Levels Series

THE SCOREBOARD

FIRST TEST: 6–11 June (Old Trafford)
Australia won by 159 runs
Australia 357 and 220
England 165 and 253

SECOND TEST: 20–25 June (Lord's)
Match Drawn
England 351
Australia 78 and 4 for 127

THIRD TEST: 11–15 July (Edgbaston)
Match Drawn
England 409 and 3 for 142
England 222 and 1 for 68

FOURTH TEST: 25–30 July (Headingley)
Match Drawn
Australia 315 and 312
England 302 and 4 for 230

FIFTH TEST: 22–27 August (The Oval)
England won by 226 runs
England 494 and 181
Australia 324 and 125

FACEBOOK MOMENT

At the Oval, staff and spectators mopped up the ground after a storm flooded the playing area, Derek Underwood did the rest taking 7 for 50 as Australia lost their last five wickets for 15 runs.

FOR THE RECORD

Most Runs:	JH Edrich (ENG) 554
Most Wickets:	AN Connolly (AUS) 23
Highest Score:	JH Edrich (ENG) 164 (Fifth Test)
Best Bowling:	DL Underwood (ENG) 7 for 50 (Fifth Test)
Most Catches:	RM Cowper (AUS) 7
Highest Run Partnership:	AP Sheahan/IM Chappell (AUS) 152 (First Test, 5th wicket)

Centuries:

England	**Australia**
MC Cowdrey	WM Lawry
JH Edrich	
BL D'Oliveira	

TWITTER FACT

Tom Graveney and Barry Jarman captained their countries for the first and only time in the Fourth Test at Headingley.

DID YOU KNOW?

Basil D'Oliveira was initially not selected in the England team to tour South Africa announced after the 1968 Ashes. When Tom Cartwright was declared unfit, England selected the South African-born batsman leading to the cancellation of the tour and a watershed moment in the sporting boycott against Apartheid.

Chapter 9

THE 1970s

Geoffrey Boycott, England

1970–71
IN AUSTRALIA

AUSTRALIA	V	ENGLAND
WM LAWRY (1–6) IM CHAPPELL (7)		R ILLINGWORTH
WON	DRAWN	WON
0	4	2

England won back the Ashes for the first time since 1953 largely through the canny captaincy of Ray Illingworth, the fiery bowling of John Snow and the slow, methodical and brilliant batting of Geoff Boycott. The good news for Australia was the unearthing of Rod Marsh, Greg Chappell and Dennis Lillee. In the First Test in Brisbane, Keith Stackpole scored a defiant 207, surviving a run out appeal when only 18. Doug Walters made 112 as Australia reached 433 (although they lost their last seven wickets for 15 runs). John Snow's 6 for 114 was a sign of what was to come. England's 464 saw all batsman contribute. Ken Shuttleworth's 5 for 47 on debut reduced Australia to 214. The first ever Test Match at the WACA in Perth also ended in a draw. England piled on 397 as Brian Luckhurst scored a ton. In just his second Test Greg Chappell scored a debut Test hundred while Ian Redpath made 171 in Australia's 440. A John Edrich undefeated 115 meant Australia needed 245 in 145 minutes and finished at 3 for 100. After the Melbourne Test was abandoned due to rain England comprehensively defeated Australia in Sydney. Geoff Boycott's unconquered 142 in the second innings and John Snow's 7 for 40 closed out the win. Bill Lawry carried his bat for 60 as Australia collapsed to 116. Bob Willis made his Test debut after being flown out to replace the injured Alan Ward. An additional Test was organised after the Third Test wash out. Australia, with the help of Ian Chappell (111) and Marsh, made 9 declared for 493. Lawry's declaration also deprived Marsh of a possible hundred and becoming the first Australian keeper to hit a Test century. Luckhurst made three figures (109) for the second time in the series while Basil D'Oliveira also scored a ton (117) in the drawn encounter. Lillee debuted in the Adelaide Test taking 5 for 84 in England's 470 in which Edrich scored 130. Illingworth didn't bother enforcing the follow-on when Australia fell for 235. A Boycott century set Australia 469 runs to win. Ian Chappell and Stackpole scored hundreds as Australia finished at 3 for 328. Chappell replaced the sacked Bill Lawry as captain in the final encounter at Sydney and invited England to bat. The move looked an astute one when England were all out for 184. Australia finished its first innings 80 runs ahead and set 223 to win. England were without Snow after the first wicket (he injured his finger colliding with the boundary fence) but dismissed the home side for 160, winning by 62 runs.

NEWSPAPER HEADLINE

Snow, Boycott Lead England to Ashes Win

THE SCOREBOARD

FIRST TEST: 27 November–2 December (Brisbane)
Match Drawn
Australia 433 and 214
England 464 and 1 for 39

SECOND TEST: 11–16 December (Perth)
Match Drawn
England 397 and 6 for 287
Australia 440 and 3 for 100

THIRD TEST: 31 December 1970–5 January, 1971 (Melbourne)
Match abandoned without a ball being bowled.

FOURTH TEST: 9–14 January (Sydney)

England won by 299 runs

England 332 and 5 for 319

Australia 236 and 116

FIFTH TEST: 21–26 January (Melbourne)

Match Drawn

Australia 493 and 4 dec. for 169

England 392 and 0 for 161

SIXTH TEST: 29 January–3 February (Adelaide)

Match Drawn

England 470 and 4 for 233

Australia 235 and 3 for 328

SEVENTH TEST: 12–17 February (Sydney)

England won by 62 runs

England 184 and 302

Australia 264 and 160

FACEBOOK MOMENT

England's fast bowler John Snow's devastating 7 for 40 in bowling Australia out for 116 in the Fourth Test at Sydney secured England's victory.

FOR THE RECORD

Most Runs:	G Boycott (ENG) 657	
Most Wickets:	JA Snow (ENG) 31	
Highest Score:	KR Stackpole (AUS) 207 (First Test)	
Best Bowling:	JA Snow (ENG) 7 for 40 (Third Test)	
Most Catches:	K R Stackpole (AUS) 9	
Highest Run	IR Redpath/GS Chappell (AUS) 219	
Partnership:	(Second Test, 6th wicket)	
Centuries:	**England**	**Australia**
	G Boycott (2)	IM Chappell (2)
	JH Edrich (2)	GS Chappell
	BL D'Oliveira	IR Redpath
	BW Luckhurst (2)	KR Stackpole (2)
		KD Walters

TWITTER FACT

Ray Illingworth led his team from the field after a section of the crowd displayed anger at John Snow who had hit tailender Terry Jenner in the head with a short-pitched ball.

DID YOU KNOW?

After the Third Test at Melbourne was abandoned without a ball being bowled, a quickly arranged limited overs match was played on what would have been the final day of the Test. Australia won the 40 over contest by five wickets in what is recognised as the first one-day international.

1972
IN ENGLAND

ENGLAND	V	AUSTRALIA
R ILLINGWORTH		IM CHAPPELL
WON	DRAWN	WON
2	1	2

Australia's period of resurgence under the captaincy of Ian Chappell was born during the 1972 Ashes. Ray Illingworth, at the age of 40, led England to a win at Old Trafford by 89 runs. Tony Greig's debut was notable, scoring two half centuries and four second innings wickets. Dennis Lillee and John Snow both took eight wickets for the match. Ian Chappell's first win as captain was during 'Massie's Match', where WA swing bowler Bob Massie took a record 16 for 137 in his Test debut. Australia's first innings 308 was bolstered by a masterly 131 from Greg Chappell. At Trent Bridge Ross Edwards, in just his second Test appearance, scored an undefeated 170 setting England 451 runs in 569 minutes to win. Brian Luckhurst batted for more than five hours for a defiant 96 as England ended the match at 4 for 290. A fusarium fungus outbreak at Headingley caused a grassless and uneven wicket most suited to spin bowling, enabling Derek Underwood's ten wickets for the match. Edwards made a pair and Australia crumbled to 146 and 136, with the match completed in three days. The squaring of the rubber at The Oval was the moment when Australian cricket asserted itself. Lillee's ten-wickets for the match and the Chappell brothers' centuries, (201 run, third wicket stand) set up a ten wicket win. Lillee and Rod Marsh created Ashes records for a tour of England with 31 wickets and 23 dismissals.

NEWSPAPER HEADLINE

'Fusarium Series' Ends in Draw

THE SCOREBOARD

FIRST TEST: 8–13 June Old Trafford
England won by 89 runs
England 249 and 234
Australia 142 and 252

SECOND TEST: 22–26 June (Lord's)
Australia won by 8 wickets
England 272 and 116
Australia 308 and 2 for 81

THIRD TEST: 13–18 July (Trent Bridge)
Match Drawn
Australia 315 and 4 for 324
England 189 and 4 for 290

FOURTH TEST: 27–29 July (Headingley)
England won by 9 wickets
Australia 146 and 136
England 263 and 1 for 21

FIFTH TEST: 10–16 August (The Oval)
Australia won by 5 wickets
England 284 and 356
Australia 399 and 5 for 242

FACEBOOK MOMENT

The double century partnership from the Chappell brothers in the
Fifth Test, set Australia up for a total of 399 in response to England's
first innings 284. This stand, along with Lillee's ten wickets for the
match, enabled Australia to level the series.

FOR THE RECORD

Most Runs:	KR Stackpole (AUS) 485
Most Wickets:	DK Lillee (AUS) 31
Highest Score:	R Edwards (AUS) 170 not out (Third Test)
Best Bowling:	RAL Massie (AUS) 8 for 53 (Second Test)
Most Catches:	GS Chappell (AUS), AW Greig (ENG) 8
Highest Run	IM Chappell, GS Chappell (AUS) 201
Partnership:	(Fifth Test, 3rd wicket,)
Centuries:	**Australia**
	IM Chappell
	GS Chappell
	R Edwards
	KR Stackpole

TWITTER FACT

No Englishman scored a Test century in the series (highest score from Brian Luckhurst with 96).

DID YOU KNOW?

The Australian cricket team had a Top 40 single with 'Here Come the Aussies' written by British pop singer Daniel Boone.

IAN CHAPPELL, AUSTRALIA

1974-75
IN AUSTRALIA

AUSTRALIA	V	ENGLAND
IM CHAPPELL		MH DENNESS (1–3,5–6) JH EDRICH (4)
WON	DRAWN	WON
4	1	1

Australia dominated England because of the fast bowling duo of Dennis Lillee and Jeff Thomson and the wonderful catching that accompanied it. Tony Greig (110) was the only centurion in the Brisbane Test as England was swept away for 265 and 166. Thomson's second innings 6 for 46, the key factor. Australia continued its winning form in Perth with Ross Edwards and Doug Walters scoring majestic hundreds (Walters scoring a 100 in a session, with a six off the last ball of the day from Bob Willis). Dennis Amiss' second innings 90 helped England set Australia 246 runs to win at the MCG. The home side finished eight runs short with just two wickets in hand. John Edrich led England at Sydney as Mike Denness dropped himself for poor form. Australia won the one-sided contest and the Ashes when off spinner Ashley Mallett had Geoff Arnold caught at short leg. Greg Chappell's second innings of 144 had set Australia up for victory. The Adelaide Test lost its first day due to rain and problems with covers being blown away, but Australia still managed to win with more than a session to spare (and despite the fact Jeff Thomson injured his shoulder playing tennis on the rest day!). Alan Knott had a memorable match scoring a century and becoming the second wicketkeeper to reach 200 dismissals. Derek Underwood took 11 of Australia's 15 wickets to fall. Dennis Amiss made his second Test pair as he continued to struggle against the pace and wile of Lillee. With Australia without the services of Thomson and Lillee (injured after 6 overs), England gained its only win of the series. Peter Lever's 6 for 38 bowled Australia out for 152. Denness finally struck form with 188 and Keith Fletcher also made a hundred (146) as England scored 529 to help them to an innings win.

NEWSPAPER HEADLINE

Lillee and Thomson Win Ashes for Aussies

THE SCOREBOARD

FIRST TEST: 29 November–4 December (Brisbane)
Australia won by 166 runs
Australia 309 and 5 dec. for 288
England 265 and 166

SECOND TEST: 13–17 December (Perth)
Australia won by 9 wickets
England 208 and 293
Australia 481 and 1 for 23

THIRD TEST: 26–31 December (Melbourne)
Match Drawn
England 242 and 244
Australia 241 and 8 for 238

FOURTH TEST: 4–9 January (Sydney)
Australia won by 171 runs
Australia 405 and 4 for 289
England 295 and 228

FIFTH TEST: 25–30 January (Adelaide)
Australia won by 163 runs
Australia 304 and 5 for 272
England 172 and 241

SIXTH TEST: 8–13 February (Melbourne)
England won by an innings and 4 runs
Australia 152 and 373
England 529

FACEBOOK MOMENT

Jeff Thomson's 6 for 46 in the second innings of the First Test
provided the killer blow to England's morale with bowling of extreme
and intimidating pace.

FOR THE RECORD

Most Runs: GS Chappell (AUS) 608
Most Wickets: JR Thomson (AUS) 33
Highest Score: MH Denness (ENG) 188 (Sixth Test)
Best Bowling: MHN Walker (AUS) 8 for 143 (Sixth Test)
Most Catches: GS Chappell (AUS) 14
Highest Run   IR Redpath/GS Chappell (AUS) 220
Partnership: (Fourth Test, 2nd wicket)
Centuries:

England	Australia
MH Denness	GS Chappell (2)
KWR Fletcher	R Edwards
AW Greig	IR Redpath
APE Knott	K D Walters

TWITTER FACT

Perth marked the return of 42-year-old off spinner Fred Titmus, who
debuted for England in 1955. It was his first Test since losing four
toes in a boating accident in the West Indies.

DID YOU KNOW?

Colin Cowdrey was called up for his sixth tour of England, finishing
his 114 Test career with 7,624 runs including 22 centuries and 120
catches.

1975
IN ENGLAND

ENGLAND	V	AUSTRALIA
MH DENNESS (1) AW GREIG (2–4)		IM CHAPPELL

WON	DRAWN	WON
0	3	1

Played at the completion of the inaugural World Cup, the four match
Test series began disastrously for England when skipper Mike
Denness elected to bowl first. Australia produced 359 but then the
home side found itself on a rain-affected pitch and were bowled out
twice for 101 and 173. Max Walker's five first innings wickets and Jeff
Thomson's second innings haul delivered a pair for debutante Graham
Gooch and a win by an innings and 85 runs for the Australians. At
Lord's, the bespectacled and grey-haired David Steele debuted with
50, England's new skipper Tony Greig fell just four runs short of a
century while Jeff Thomson bowled 22 no balls in the home side's first
innings. John Edrich's 175 saw England to 7 for 436 before Australia
batted out for a draw. The hope of an exciting finish at Headingley
was ruined when protestors campaigning for the release of a prisoner
(George Davis) vandalised the pitch. Australia was 3 for 220 chasing
445 to win on the final day. McCosker was 95 and in pursuit of his
first Test hundred when the match was called off. England followed-
on at The Oval after an Ian Chappell (192) and McCosker (127) led
the way for Australia as they reached 9 declared for 532 and bowled
England out for 191.Bob Woolmer in only his second Test made 149
in more than eight hours in what was the longest first-class match
played in England, covering six days.

NEWSPAPER HEADLINE

Aussies On Top In Short Series

THE SCOREBOARD

FIRST TEST: 10–14 July (Edgbaston)
Australia won by an innings and 85 runs
Australia 359
England 101 and 173

SECOND TEST: 31 July–5 August (Lord's)
Match Drawn
England 315 and 7 dec. for 436
Australia 268 and 3 for 329

THIRD TEST: 14–19 August (Headingley)
Match Drawn
England 288 and 291
Australia 135 and 3 for 220

FOURTH TEST: 28 August–3 September (The Oval)
Match Drawn
Australia 532 and 2 for 40
England 191 and 538

FACEBOOK MOMENT

When England captain Mike Denness sent Australia into bat at Edgbaston it gave the visitors best use of the pitch. England then had to bat twice on a rain-affected pitch and were bowled out cheaply. Denness was dropped as captain and replaced by the more aggressive and pragmatic Tony Greig.

FOR THE RECORD

Most Runs:	IM Chappell (AUS) 429
Most Wickets:	DK Lillee (AUS) 21
Highest Score:	IM Chappell (AUS) 193 (Fifth Test)
Best Bowling:	DK Lillee (AUS) 5 for 15 (First Test)
Most Catches:	GS Chappell (AUS) 9
Highest Run Partnership:	RB McCosker/IM Chappell (AUS) 277 (Fifth Test, 2nd wicket)

Centuries:

England	**Australia**
JH Edrich	IM Chappell
RA Woolmer	RB McCosker

TWITTER FACT

Australian leg spinner Jim Higgs did not score a run and was out to the only ball he received on tour (against Leicestershire where he was also no balled for throwing).

DID YOU KNOW?

England commentator John Arlott described Lord's first streaker as a 'freaker' as Michale Angelow (a cook in the Merchant Navy) hurdled each set of stumps on the fourth afternoon of the Second Test.

1977
IN ENGLAND

ENGLAND	V	AUSTRALIA
JM BREARLEY		GS CHAPPELL
WON	DRAWN	WON
3	2	0

It was always going to be a challenging tour for the Australians in 1977. The Jubilee Test which celebrated 25 years of the reign of Queen Elizabeth II lost almost six hours because of rain. After England was bowled out for 216, Craig Serjeant, on debut, managed 81 despite Bob Willis's barnstorming 7 for 78. Woolmer delivered his second consecutive hundred in England's first innings at Old Trafford. Derek Underwood's six second innings wickets, the last time he took five or more wickets in an innings in a Test in England, bowled Australia out for 218. Greg Chappell provided a masterclass of batting with 112. England won the match by nine wickets with Dennis Amiss in his final innings in Test cricket against Australia ending with an undefeated 28.

Geoff Boycott's reintroduction to Test cricket after missing 30 matches succeeded with 107, Alan Knott's 135 took him past 4000 runs in Test cricket (his counterpart Rod Marsh scored a pair). Debutante Ian Botham's first innings five wicket haul dismissed the visitors for 243 in the first innings while Bob Willis was the second innings destroyer with 5 for 88. England chased down the winning runs with only three wickets down, after Mike Brearley and Boycott put on 154 for the second innings. Boycott's 100th first-class hundred during his home ground Headingley Test helped England to 436. He was last out for 191 having batted for 629 minutes. Botham's first innings 5 for 21 put the final nail in Australia's coffin as they were bowled out for 103 and 248. Rain again interrupted play at The Oval with almost two days lost. Greig scored a duck in his final innings for

England as Australia took the early stronghold bowling the home side out for 214. David Hookes made his highest Ashes score of 85 out of Australia's 385 in the drawn match.

NEWSPAPER HEADLINE

Boycott, Botham Head England Triumph

THE SCOREBOARD

FIRST TEST: 16–21 June (Lord's)
Match Drawn
England 216 and 305
Australia 296 and 6 for 114

SECOND TEST: 7–12 July (Old Trafford)
England won by 9 wickets
Australia 297 and 218
England 437 and 1 for 82

THIRD TEST: 28 July–2 August (Trent Bridge)
England won by 7 wickets
Australia 243 and 309
England 364 and 3 for 189

FOURTH TEST; 11–15 August (Headingley)
England won by an innings and 85 runs
England 436
Australia 103 and 248

FIFTH TEST: 25–30 August (The Oval)
Match Drawn
England 214 and 2 for 57
Australia 385

FACEBOOK MOMENT

On May 9, it was revealed that Australian businessman Kerry Packer had signed up the cream of Test cricket talent from around the world to create his own series of matches. Thirteen of Australia's touring party of 17 were signed creating a great unrest as the party divided into two distinct parts.

FOR THE RECORD

Most Runs:	G Boycott (ENG) 442
Most Wickets:	RGD Willis (ENG) 27
Highest Score:	G Boycott (ENG) 191 (Fourth Test)
Best Bowling:	RGD Willis (ENG) 7 for 78 (First Test)
Most Catches:	AW Greig (ENG) 9
Highest Run Partnership:	G Boycott/APE Knott (ENG) 215 (Third Test, 6th wicket)

Centuries:	**England**	**Australia**
	G Boycott (2)	GS Chappell
	APE Knott	RB McCosker
	RA Woolmer (2)	

TWITTER FACT

Australia finished the tour with just five first-class wins out of 22 matches.

DID YOU KNOW?

The return of England opening batsman Geoffrey Boycott, who had been in self-imposed exile for 30 matches, was striking. In the three Tests, he played he averaged 147 after scoring 442 runs.

1978-79
IN AUSTRALIA

AUSTRALIA	v	ENGLAND
GN YALLOP		JM BREARLEY
WON	DRAWN	WON
1		5

Played in the shadow of Kerry Packer's first season of World Series Cricket, England easily won the 1978–79 Ashes against a largely depleted Australian side. With Australia bowled out for 116 on the first day of the Test opener at Brisbane, England set the tone for the series. Graham Yallop and Kim Hughes' maiden Ashes Test hundreds demonstrated signs of an Australian comeback but it wasn't enough, although Rodney Hogg's 6 for 74 in the first innings was an indication as to what was to come. David Gower's 102 and Geoffrey Boycott's 77 (seven and a half hours) set England up with a first innings 309 in the Second Test at Perth. Bob Willis' 5 for 44 bowled Australia out for 190, despite a gallant undefeated 81 from Peter Toohey. Australia's only win for the series took place at Melbourne where a 115 run lead on the first innings held sway. Graeme Wood's even 100 bolstered Australia's first innings 258 as England tumbled to 143. Hogg's ten wickets for the match ensured a 103 run win. Derek Randall's 150 consuming 582 minutes provided the turning point of the Sydney Test (despite protestations that Randall was out LBW third ball). Australia's 142 run first innings lead (Rick Darling 91) meant little when they fell for 111 in the second innings. England had retained the Ashes for the first time in Australia since 1954–55. A first innings England collapse to 169 at Adelaide gave Australia false hope. They were bowled out five runs in arrears in a 205 run loss. A final nine wicket win by England rounded out the series at the SCG.

NEWSPAPER HEADLINE

England Win 5–1 Over Packer-Depleted Aussies

THE SCOREBOARD

FIRST TEST: 1–6 December (Brisbane)
England won by 7 wickets
Australia 116 and 339
England 286 and 3 for 170

SECOND TEST: 15–20 December (Perth)
England won by 166 runs
England 309 and 208
Australia 190 and 161

THIRD TEST: 29 December–3 January (Melbourne)
Australia won by 103 runs
Australia 258 and 167
England 143 and 179

FOURTH TEST: 6–11 January (Sydney)
England won by 93 runs
England 152 and 346
Australia 294 and 111

FIFTH TEST: 27 January–1 February (Adelaide)
England won by 205 runs
England 169 and 360
Australia 164 and 160

SIXTH TEST: 10–14 February (Sydney)
England won by 9 wickets
Australia 198 and 143
England 308

FACEBOOK MOMENT

Australian umpire Tom Brooks announced his retirement during the Perth Test after criticism about some controversial decisions.

FOR THE RECORD

Most Runs:	D I Gower (ENG) 420
Most Wickets:	RM Hogg (AUS) 41
Highest Score:	DW Randall (ENG) 150 (Fourth Test)
Best Bowling:	RM Hogg (AUS) 6 for 74 (First Test)
Most Catches:	IT Botham (ENG) 11
Highest Run	GN Yallop/KJ Hughes (AUS) 170
Partnership:	(Fourth Test, 4th wicket)

Centuries:	**England**	**Australia**
	DI Gower	KJ Hughes
	DW Randall	GM Wood
		DN Yallop (2)

TWITTER FACT

The nerve wracking running between the wickets between Graeme Wood and Rick Darling was so poor they were nicknamed the Kamikaze Kids.

DID YOU KNOW?

As Test cricket continued its battle for supremacy over Kerry Packer's World Series Cricket, the record low attendance at the Sixth Test at Sydney, of 22,617 for the match was the worst since 1888.

CHAPTER 10

THE 1980s

1981
IN ENGLAND

ENGLAND	V	AUSTRALIA
IT BOTHAM (1–2) JM BREARLEY (3–5)		KJ HUGHES
WON	**DRAWN**	**WON**
3	2	1

In the absence of Greg Chappell, Kim Hughes captained Australia in
what was one of the most exciting and surprising Ashes series of the
modern era. At Trent Bridge Australia won a low scoring encounter
by 4 wickets. Allan Border's first innings 63, the highest score of
the match. A drawn Test at Lord's, after Hughes decided to send
England in to bat in consecutive matches. Geoff Lawson's 7 for 81
reduced England to 311, when the home side lost their last 6 wickets
for 27. Ian Botham's pair contributing to his decision to resign before
facing the sack ending his 12 match reign. Headingley delivered one
of the most amazing matches of all time providing England with its
first win in 13 Tests. It was the Bob Willis and Ian Botham shows as
having followed-on England scored 356 and bowled Australia out for
111. Willis took 8 for 43 while Botham helped set up the unexpected
victory with 6 first innings wickets and an undefeated 149 (including
a ton off 87 balls) in the second. History repeated at Edgbaston
where Australia was bowled out again cheaply, this time for 121 in
pursuit of a small total and lost by 29 runs. Botham's spell of 5 for 1
in 28 balls helping Australia lose its last 6 wickets for just 16 runs.
Despite Australia's sizable second innings of 402, they fell 103 runs
short after giving England a 101 run first innings lead in the Fifth
Test at Old Trafford. Botham set England alight again with 118, his
second hundred of the series, while Alan Knott took his number of
dismissals against Australia to 100. Old adversaries Boycott (137)
and Lillee (7 for 89) went head-to-head for the last time with the Oval
Test ending in a draw and giving England a memorable series, 3–1.

NEWSPAPER HEADLINE

Botham's Ashes!

THE SCOREBOARD

FIRST TEST: 18–21 June (Trent Bridge)
Australia won by 4 wickets
England 185 and 125
Australia 179 and 6 for 132

SECOND TEST: 2–7 July (Lord's)
Match Drawn
England 311 and 8 for 265
Australia 345 and 4 for 90

THIRD TEST: 16–21 July (Headingley)
England won by 18 runs
Australia 401 and 111
England 174 and 356

FOURTH TEST: 30 July–2 August (Edgbaston)
England won by 29 runs
England 189 and 219
Australia 258 and 121

FIFTH TEST: 13–17 August (Old Trafford)
England won by 103 runs
England 231 and 404
Australia 130 and 402

SIXTH TEST: 27 August–1 September (The Oval)
Match Drawn
Australia 352 and 9 dec. for 344
England 314 and 7 for 261

FACEBOOK MOMENT

At Headingley, when Ian Botham and Graham Dilley added 117 for the eighth wicket it signalled a comeback that was completed when Ray Bright was bowled by Bob Willis to give victory to England by 18 runs. This was after England had followed-on after scoring 174 in response to Australia's 401.

FOR THE RECORD

Most Runs:	AR Border (AUS) 533	
Most Wickets:	TM Alderman (AUS) 42	
Highest Score:	IT Botham (ENG) 149 (Third Test)	
Best Bowling:	RGD Willis (ENG) 8 for 43 (Third Test)	
Most Catches:	AR Border (AUS), IT Botham (ENG) 12	
Highest Run	CJ Tavare/IT Botham (ENG) 149	
Partnership:	(Fifth Test, 6th wicket)	
Centuries:	**England**	**Australia**
	IT Botham (2)	AR Border (2)
	G Boycott	J Dyson
		DM Wellham
		GN Yallop

TWITTER FACT

When Trevor Chappell was selected for the First Test at Trent Bridge it marked the first time that three brothers had represented Australia in Tests.

DID YOU KNOW?

Rod Marsh and Dennis Lillee placed bets on Australia losing when they saw the odds of 500–1 at the tea break on the fourth day as a bit of a joke. When Australia lost the match, and Marsh and Lillee won the bet, they bought the team's English bus driver, Peter Tribe a man they called 'The Geezer' a set of golf clubs and a return air ticket to Australia.

1982–83
IN AUSTRALIA

AUSTRALIA	V	ENGLAND
GS CHAPPELL		RGD WILLIS
WON	DRAWN	WON
2	2	1

A tour where England was without some of its best players including
Graham Gooch, Geoff Boycott, John Emburey, Derek Underwood and
Alan Knott (all banned for three years for touring Apartheid South
Africa on a 'rebel' tour) leaving fast bowler Bob Willis to captain the
side. The First Test saw an invasion of spectators on the second day,
where Terry Alderman was badly injured. Bruce Yardley who had
been omitted from the 1981 Australian team to England toiled for 5
for 107 in England's first innings 411. Australia was too strong at the
Gabba, after Geoff Lawson's 6 for 47 bowled England out for 219. South
African-born Kepler Wessels started his Test career for Australia with
162, having been dropped at 15. Kim Hughes and David Hookes with
a partnership of 107 took Australia to victory. Willis invited Australia
to bat on a perfect pitch at Adelaide Oval and Greg Chappell scored his
second century of the series as the home side mounted a score of 438.
At 3 for 181, England looked primed for a big total before collapsing
to be all out for 216. England won a dramatic Test at Melbourne after
being sent into bat and scoring a first innings 284. England's South
African-born player Allan Lamb scoring 83 (his second score in the 80s
in consecutive Tests). Hughes' 66 and Hookes' 53 led Australia to a
three run lead. Norman Cowans' six wickets reduced Australia to 9 for
218 but the home side fell four runs short when Thomson was caught
by Miller off Botham. A drawn encounter at Sydney meant Australia
regained the Ashes after a five-year hiatus. Hughes's second innings
137 and English off spinner Eddie Hemmings' 95 (after going into bat
as a night watchman), the highlights.

IAN BOTHAM, BOB TAYLOR AND GRAHAM GOOCH, ENGLAND

NEWSPAPER HEADLINE

Ashes Return to Australia

THE SCOREBOARD

FIRST TEST: 12–17 November (Brisbane)
Match Drawn
England 411 and 358
Australia 9 dec. for 424 and 2 for 73

SECOND TEST: 26 November–1 December (Perth)
Australia won by 7 wickets
England 219 and 309
Australia 341 and 3 for 190

THIRD TEST: 10–15 December (Adelaide)
Australia won by 8 wickets
Australia 438 and 2 for 83
England 216 and 304

FOURTH TEST: 26–30 December (Melbourne)
England won by 3 runs
England 284 and 294
Australia 287 and 288

FIFTH TEST: 3–7 January (Sydney)
Match Drawn
Australia 314 and 382
England 237 and 7 for 314

FACEBOOK MOMENT

England captain Bob Willis sent Australia into bat on a beautiful
wicket at Adelaide, just the third England captain to do so. Australia
scored 438 and bowled England out for 216 with Australia gaining an
unassailable lead.

GREG CHAPPELL, AUSTRALIA

FOR THE RECORD

Most Runs:	KJ Hughes (AUS) 469
Most Wickets:	GF Lawson (AUS) 34
Highest Score:	KC Wessels (AUS) 162 (Second Test)
Best Bowling:	GF Lawson (AUS) 6 for 47 (Second Test)
Most Catches:	IT Botham (ENG) 9
Highest Run Partnership:	CJ Tavare/AJ Lamb 161 (ENG) 161 (Fourth Test, 4th wicket)

Centuries:

England	Australia
DI Gower	GS Chappell (2)
DW Randall	KJ Hughes
	KC Wessels

TWITTER FACT

Greg Chappell made his ninth and final Ashes hundred in the Third Test at the Adelaide Oval (his first at his former home ground).

DID YOU KNOW?

The Fourth Test at Melbourne showed for the first time a huge video scoreboard with replays as well as the score.

1985
IN ENGLAND

ENGLAND	V	AUSTRALIA
DI GOWER		AR BORDER
WON	DRAWN	WON
3	2	1

A one-way series for the home side. A one-way series for the home
side with Australia struggling without former captain Kim Hughes,
Graham Yallop, Terry Alderman and Rodney Hogg (ruled out because
of their involvement in the rebel South African tour). An Andrew
Hilditch double of 119 and 80 at Headingley couldn't stop England
taking out the series opener by five wickets. Australia turned the
tables at Lord's. England was twice bowled out for under 300, with
young fast bowler Craig McDermott taking five wickets in the first
innings and 35-year-old leg spinner Bob Holland five in the second.
Australian captain Allan Border fell just short of a double century,
with 196. A high scoring encounter (interrupted by rain) ended in a
draw at Trent Bridge. David Gower's 166 setting England up for 456.
Australia led on the first innings by 83 after centuries from Graeme
Wood and Greg Ritchie. Rain was also an influence at Old Trafford as
Gower put England in and bowled the visitors out for 257. McDermott
was the only Australian bowler to take a wicket with 8 for 141, as
Mike Gatting made his first Test ton in England with 160. England
took hold of the series in the final two Tests with large totals and
clever swing bowling. At Edgbaston, England's 5 declared for 595
featured a second wicket partnership of 331 between Robinson (148)
and Gower (215). Australia collapsed in the second innings for 142
with Richard Ellison adding to his six wickets in the first innings to
make it ten for the match. England rolled on to another big score at
The Oval. This time it was Graham Gooch who shared the honours
with his skipper Gower for a 351 run stand in 337 minutes. Ellison
again the main damager with 5 for 46.

NEWSPAPER HEADLINE

England's Ashes
as Gower, Ellison Shine

THE SCOREBOARD

FIRST TEST: 13–18 June (Headingley)
England won by 5 wickets
Australia 331 and 324
England 533 and 5 for 123

SECOND TEST: 27 June–2 July (Lord's)
Australia won by 4 wickets
England 290 and 261
Australia 425 and 6 for 127

THIRD TEST: 11–16 July (Trent Bridge)
Match Drawn
England 456 and 2 for 196
Australia 539

FOURTH TEST: 1–6 August (Old Trafford)
Match Drawn
Australia 257 and 5 for 340
England 482

FIFTH TEST: 15–20 August (Edgbaston)
England won by an innings and 118 runs
Australia 335 and 142
England 5 dec. for 595

SIXTH TEST: 29 August–2 September (The Oval)
England won by an innings and 94 runs
England 464
Australia 241 and 129

FACEBOOK MOMENT

Richard Ellison's 4 for 27 and Ian Botham's 3 for 52 bowled Australia out for 142 in the Fifth Test. When Wayne Phillips was controversially given out caught in short off Allan Lamb's foot, Australia's chance to hold out was lost.

FOR THE RECORD

Most Runs:	DI Gower (ENG) 732
Most Wickets:	IT Botham (ENG) 31
Highest Score:	DI Gower (ENG) 215 (Fifth Test)
Best Bowling:	CJ McDermott (AUS) 8 for 141 (Fourth Test)
Most Catches:	AR Border (AUS) 11
Highest Run	GA Gooch/DI Gower (England) 351
Partnership:	(Sixth Test, 2nd wicket)

	England	**Australia**
Centuries:	DI Gower (3)	AR Border (2)
	GA Gooch	AMJ Hilditch
	MW Gatting (2)	GM Ritchie
	RT Robinson (2)	GM Wood

TWITTER FACT

Australian fast bowler Jeff Thomson took his 200th and final wicket in Test cricket when he dismissed Gooch at Edgbaston.

DID YOU KNOW?

BBC commentator Jonathan Agnew played his only Ashes Test at Old Trafford, where he failed to take a wicket from 23 overs.

1986–87
IN AUSTRALIA

AUSTRALIA	v	ENGLAND
AR BORDER		MW GATTING
WON	DRAWN	WON
1	2	2

England maintained its stronghold over the Australian side, despite woeful form leading into the First Test. Having been sent in, England with the help of Ian Botham's 138, (including 22 from one Merv Hughes over) managed 456. Geoff Marsh batted the entire fourth day as the home side followed-on, this time off spinner John Emburey taking 5 for 80. England chased a small total winning by seven wickets. At Perth, Chris Broad and Bill Athey added 223 for the opening partnership with four England centurions (Broad, Gower, David Gower and wicketkeeper Jack Richards) in a total of 8 declared for 592. Allan Border's 125 added weight to Australia's 401 in the drawn match. The high scoring continued at Adelaide where David Boon's 103 helped Australia to 5 declared for 514. Broad's 116 and Gatting making an even century as a rain-affected final day meant a draw was a formality. England won the first three-day Ashes Test since 1901–02 at the MCG as Gladstone Small and Ian Botham accounted for the Australians for 141. Broad managed his third ton in three Tests, and Australia was bowled out for 194 with Geoff Marsh's 60, the only real sign of resistance. With the Ashes lost, Sydney provided solace for the Australia side, led by Dean Jones' 184 not out, and a total of 343. Newcomer Peter Taylor after just six first-class matches celebrated his Test debut with six wickets in England's 275. Australia at 7 for 145 looked like squandering its first innings advantage before Taylor (42) helped Steve Waugh (73) set England 320 to win. Off spinner Emburey continued his good form with 7 for 78 in the second dig but Peter Sleep's five wickets spun Australia to victory by 55 runs.

NEWSPAPER HEADLINE

England's 'Worst Team Ever' Retains Ashes

THE SCOREBOARD

FIRST TEST: 14–19 November (Brisbane)
England won by 7 wickets
England 456 and 3 for 77
Australia 248 and 282

SECOND TEST: 28 November–3 December (Perth)
Match Drawn
England 8 dec. for 592 and 8 dec. for 199
Australia 401 and 4 for 197

THIRD TEST: 12–16 December (Adelaide)
Match Drawn
Australia 5 dec. for 514 and 3 dec. 201
England 455 and 2 for 39

FOURTH TEST: 26–28 December (Melbourne)
England won by an innings and 14 runs
Australia 141 and 194
England 349

FIFTH TEST: 10–15 January (Sydney)
Australia won by 55 runs
Australia 343 and 251
England 275 and 264

FACEBOOK MOMENT

Gladstone Small's five wicket haul in bowling Australia out for 141, after he came into the side to replace Dilley, and Chris Broad's Third Test century in three Tests set England up for a three day win at the MCG.

FOR THE RECORD

Most Runs:	DM Jones (AUS) 511
Most Wickets:	BA Reid (AUS) 20
Highest Score:	DM Jones (AUS) 184 not out (Fifth Test)
Best Bowling:	JE Emburey (ENG) 7 for 78 (Fifth Test)
Most Catches:	IT Botham (ENG) 10
Highest Run	BC Broad/CWJ Athey (ENG) 223
Partnership:	(Second Test, 1st wicket)

Centuries:	**England**	**Australia**
	IT Botham	DC Boon
	BC Broad (3)	AR Border (2)
	MW Gatting	DM Jones
	DI Gower	GR Marsh
	CJ Richards	

TWITTER FACT

England had such terrible form leading into the First Test at Brisbane, they were described by English journalist Martin Johnson thus; "There are only three things wrong with this England team. They can't bat, can't bowl and can't field."

DID YOU KNOW?

When little-known New South Wales' off spinner Peter Taylor was selected to make his Test debut in the final Test at Sydney, one newspaper headline ran 'Peter Who'? Taylor rewarded the selectors with 8 wickets for the match.

1989
IN ENGLAND

ENGLAND	V	AUSTRALIA
DI GOWER		AR BORDER
WON	DRAWN	WON
O	2	4

Australia began a dominance over England that would last more than a decade. Australia's first innings 601 set the tone for the series, where Mark Taylor (136) and Steve Waugh (177 not out) scored debut Test centuries. Terry Alderman recreated some of the 1981 Ashes form with 10 wickets as Alan Lamb provided the highlight for the home team with a first innings of 125. England's second innings collapse gifted Australia a win in the opener by 210 runs. Allan Border became the first Australian to lead his team to victory at Lord's twice, helped by Steve Waugh's undefeated 152 in the first innings and Alderman's nine wicket match haul. Almost ten hours of play was lost at Edgbaston in the Second Test, where Dean Jones' 157 set Australia up for a first innings 424. England were 'Aldermanned' again (3 for 61) and fell for 242. The match finished in a draw before a nine wicket win at Old Trafford returned the Ashes to Australia. South African-born Robin Smith's 143, the shining light in England's first innings 260 as Geoff Lawson took 6 for 72. The final day also revealed that three members of the England team – John Emburey, Neil Foster and Tim Robinson – had signed a rebel South African tour contract. Australian openers Geoff Marsh (138) and Mark Taylor (219) put on 329 for the opening partnership at Trent Bridge, as Australia climbed to 603. Robin Smith scored his second century in consecutive Tests, as England managed only 255. Future England captain Michael Atherton was out second ball in his debut Test innings although made 47 as England were all out for 167 in the innings and 180 run win to Australia. At the Oval, rain reduced play on the second and third days due to rain didn't stop Australia from accumulating 468 with the 'Jones Boy' scoring his second ton of the series in the drawn encounter.

NEWSPAPER HEADLINE

Border Leads Aussie Ashes Landslide

THE SCOREBOARD

FIRST TEST: 8–13 June (Headingly)
Australia won by 210 runs
Australia 601 and 3 dec. for 230
England 430 and 191

SECOND TEST: 22–27 June (Lord's)
Australia won by 6 wickets
England 286 and 359
Australia 528 and 4 for 119

THIRD TEST: 6–11 July (Edgbaston)
Match Drawn
Australia 424 and 2 for 158
England 242

FOURTH TEST: 27 July–1 August (Old Trafford)
Australia won by 9 wickets
England 260 and 264
Australia 447 and 1 for 81

FIFTH TEST: 10–14 August (Trent Bridge)
Australia won by an innings and 180 runs
Australia 6 dec. for 602
England 255 and 167

SIXTH TEST: 24–29 August (The Oval)
Match Drawn
Australia 468 and 4 dec. for 219
England 285 and 5 for 143

FACEBOOK MOMENT

Australia's first innings 601, signalled that Australian batting held few fears of the England attack. Terry Alderman's ten wickets for the match proving he would again be a major threat.

FOR THE RECORD

Most Runs:	MA Taylor (AUS) 839
Most Wickets:	TM Alderman (AUS) 41
Highest Score:	MA Taylor (AUS) 219 (Fifth Test)
Best Bowling:	GF Lawson (AUS) 6 for 72 (Fourth Test)
Most Catches:	DC Boon (AUS) 9
Highest Run	GR Marsh/MA Taylor (AUS) 329
Partnership:	(Fifth Test, 1st wicket)

Centuries:	**England**	**Australia**
	DI Gower	GR Marsh
	AJ Lamb	DM Jones (2)
	RC Russell	MA Taylor (2)
	RA Smith (2)	SW Waugh (2)

TWITTER FACT

England used 29 players for the series while Australia, unchanged for five Tests, used just 12.

DID YOU KNOW?

When the Australian team returned to Australia they were not only welcomed by a parade in Sydney but also appeared at the MCG doing a lap of honour before the 1989 Grand Final between Hawthorn and Geelong. Off spinner Tim May cheekily held a soccer ball.

CHAPTER 11

THE 1990s

ALLAN BORDER, AUSTRALIA

1990–91
IN AUSTRALIA

AUSTRALIA	v	ENGLAND
AR BORDER		AJ LAMB (1) GA GOOCH (2–5)
WON	DRAWN	WON
3	2	0

Any psychological advantage built in the 1989 Ashes grew throughout
the summer as Australia romped to a 3–0 win. Allan Lamb captained
England in the First Test as Graham Gooch nursed his hand after
surgery. Bruce Reid and Terry Alderman made the most of the
Gabba's steaming conditions bowling England out for 194 and 114.
Alderman recorded his career best figures of 6 for 47. David Gower's
61, the only England batsman to score a half century. In Melbourne,
Gower scored the only century of the match as England made 352
in difficult conditions. All the Australian top order managed starts
with Border's 62, the highest score in its first innings of 306. The
visitors lost 6 wickets for 3 runs as Reid's seven wickets quickly
made inroads. David Boon remained on 94 not out at Australia
went two up in the rubber. Australia's spinning all-rounder Greg
Matthews scored Australia's only ton in a first innings 518 at the
SCG. England responded with 469, helped by Mike Atherton's first
Ashes hundred, while Gower continued his impressive form with
123. Phil Tufnell's left-arm tweakers, taking 5 for 61 in Australia's
205, with keeper Ian Healy's 69 providing strong support (batting at
number three as a nightwatchman.) Set 255 in under three hours,
England was 4 for 113 at the close. A debut Test century for Mark
Waugh (138 off 188 balls) in Adelaide set Australia up to score 386.
Craig McDermott's five wickets led to an early England collapse
before Gooch fell for 87. David Boon's second innings 121 helped set
the visitors 472 while Gooch's 117 saw them to a respectable 5 for

335 in the drawn match. Australia's series dominance resumed at Perth, where McDermott's 11 wickets for the match routed England for 244 and 182.

NEWSPAPER HEADLINE

Aussies Steamroll England!

THE SCOREBOARD

FIRST TEST: 23–25 November (Brisbane)
Australia won by 10 wickets
England 194 and 114
Australia 152 and 0 for 157

SECOND TEST: 26–30 December (Melbourne)
Australia won by 8 wickets
England 352 and 150
Australia 306 and 2 for 197

THIRD TEST: 4–8 January (Sydney)
Match Drawn
Australia 518 and 205
England 469 and 4 for 113

FOURTH TEST: 25–29 January (Adelaide)
Match Drawn
Australia 386 and 6 dec. for 314
England 229 and 5 for 335

FIFTH TEST: 1–5 February (Perth)
Australia won by 9 wickets
England 244 and 182
Australia 307 and 1 for 120

FACEBOOK MOMENT

Bruce Reid's best Ashes analysis of 13 wickets for 148, mowed England down for a second innings 150 resulting in an eight wicket win at the MCG. Australia was suddenly 2–0 up in the series.

FOR THE RECORD

Most Runs:	DC Boon (AUS) 530
Most Wickets:	BA Reid (AUS) 27
Highest Score:	ME Waugh (AUS) 138 (Fourth Test)
Best Bowling:	CJ Mc Dermott (AUS) 8 for 97 (Fifth Test)
Most Catches:	MA Taylor (AUS) 8
Highest Run	GA Gooch/MA Atherton (ENG) 203
Partnership:	(Fourth Test, 1st wicket)

Centuries:	**England**	**Australia**
	MA Atherton	DC Boon
	GA Gooch	GJ Matthews
	DI Gower (2)	ME Waugh

TWITTER FACT

Phil Tufnell, despite not taking a wicket in his debut Test in 45 overs, almost took a hat-trick in his next match at the SCG, in a five wicket haul.

DID YOU KNOW?

David Gower was fined £1000 after he and teammate John Morris hired a Tiger Moth and flew over the Carrara ground to celebrate Robin Smith's century.

1993
IN ENGLAND

ENGLAND	V	AUSTRALIA
GA GOOCH (1–5)		AR BORDER
MA ATHERTON (6)		
WON	DRAWN	WON
1	1	4

1993 was a series defined by 'that ball', a delivery that young Australian leg spinner Shane Warne bowled to dismiss Mike Gatting in the First Test at Old Trafford. Warne's eight wickets for the match, saw Australia register a 179 run win. Mark Taylor (124) continued his England dominance away from home while Ian Healy made his maiden Test ton. Graham Gooch's second innings 133 ended in the unlikely manner of 'handling the ball' as Australia won with just under ten overs remaining. Australia's indomitable 632 first innings total at Lord's set the tone for the match. Mark Waugh, on 99, was the only batsman in Australia's top four to miss out on a century (Taylor 111, Michael Slater 152, David Boon 164 not out). Border completed his Test record at Lord's with 77 taking his Test average there to 100. Warne and off spinner Tim May bowled England out twice as Australia continued its winning form at the spiritual home of cricket. At Trent Bridge, England introduced four debutantes, including opening bowlers Martin McCague and Mark Ilott. Australia were set the unlikely target of 371 in a minimum 77 overs but never really gave chase resulting in a draw. Border (with his first Ashes century in six years with 200 not out) and Waugh added an unbroken 332 at Headingley while England totalled 505 across two innings. Gooch resigned the captaincy as England slumped to an innings and 148 run loss. Mark Waugh scored Australia's tenth hundred of the series at Edgbaston while Warne and May added the finishing touches to the demoralisation of England as Australia romped to an eight wicket win. England finally snatched a victory at The Oval with their West Indian-born bowler Devon Malcolm making the Australian top order at the crease.

NEWSPAPER HEADLINE

Aussies Cruise as Ashes Retained

THE SCOREBOARD

FIRST TEST: 3–7 June (Old Trafford)
Australia won by 179 runs
Australia 289 and 5 dec. for 432
England 210 and 332

SECOND TEST: 17–21 June (Lord's)
Australia won by an innings and 62 runs
Australia 4 dec. for 632
England 205 and 365

THIRD TEST: 1–6 July (Trent Bridge)
Match Drawn
England 321 and 6 dec. for 422
Australia 373 and 6 for 202

FOURTH TEST: 22–26 July (Headingley)
Australia won by an innings and 148 runs
Australia 4 dec. for 653
England 200 and 305

FIFTH TEST: 5–9 August (Edgbaston)
Australia won by 8 wickets
England 276 and 251
Australia 408 and 2 for 120

SIXTH TEST: 19–22 August (The Oval)
England won by 161 runs
England 380 and 313
Australia 303 and 229

FACEBOOK MOMENT

The Shane Warne delivery, the first ball he bowled in Ashes cricket dubbed 'the ball of the century' at Old Trafford. It deceived Mike Gatting and sent a shiver down the spine of every England batsman.

FOR THE RECORD

Most Runs: G Gooch (ENG) 673
Most Wickets: SK Warne (AUS) 34
Highest Score: AR Border (AUS) 200 not out (Fourth Test)
Best Bowling: P Such (ENG) 6 for 67 (First Test)
Most Catches: M Taylor (AUS) 11
Highest Run   A R Border/SR Waugh (AUS) 332
Partnership: (Fourth Test, 5th wicket)

Centuries:	**England**	**Australia**
	GA Gooch (2)	AR Border
	GF Thorpe	DC Boon (3)
		IA Healy
		MJ Slater
		MA Taylor
		ME Waugh
		SR Waugh (2)

TWITTER FACT

Australia's spin pair of Shane Warne and Tim May took a record 55 wickets between them in this series.

DID YOU KNOW?

The Sixth Test at The Oval was to be the last for much-loved English commentator Brian Johnston, who died in January of 1994. He had commentated on the BBC for 48 years.

1994–95
IN AUSTRALIA

AUSTRALIA	v	ENGLAND
MA TAYLOR		MA ATHERTON
WON	DRAWN	WON
3	1	1

In the First Test at Brisbane, Warne took three wickets in four balls
during a second innings rout of 8 for 71. Michael Slater's first innings
176 and Mark Waugh's 140, (his 50th first-class century) provided
the foundation for Australia's 184 run win. Warne then passed 150
wickets in Test cricket with a first innings 6 for 64 at the MCG. Amid
low scoring first innings Australia led after David Boon's 131 in the
second. Darren Gough's seven wickets for the match giving England
some signs of hope but the visitors were swept away for 92 in just 42
overs, with Warne taking the first hat-trick in Ashes cricket since
1903–04. England had the early upper hand in Sydney. Gough's 6 for
49 routed the Australians for 116 although they narrowly avoided the
follow-on. Atherton infamously declared at 2 for 255, with Graham
Hick on 98, starving him of what would have been his only Ashes ton.
Adelaide fans witnessed a crawling century from Gatting, spending
more than half an hour on 99 as England mounted an impressive 353.
Debutante Greg Blewett became the first South Australia batsman to
score a ton on debut at Adelaide Oval as Australia mounted a 66 run
first innings lead. A thrilling finish ensued after England all-rounder
Phil DeFreitas scored 88 and set Australia 263 to win. England's
pace duo of Devon Malcolm and Chris Lewis bowled Australia out
with just 35 balls to spare. Australia's stronghold over England was
complete at Perth when another Slater ton took him past 600 runs for
the series. Steve Waugh was left stranded on 99 in Australia's first
innings of 402.

NEWSPAPER HEADLINE

Aussies Counter
Injury-plagued England

THE SCOREBOARD

FIRST TEST: 25–29 November (Brisbane)
Australia won by 184 runs
Australia 426 and 8 dec. for 248
England 167 and 323

SECOND TEST: 24–20 December (Melbourne)
Australia won by 295 runs
Australia 279 and 7 dec. for 320
England 212 and 92

THIRD TEST: 1–5 January (Sydney)
Match Drawn
England 309 2 dec. for 255
Australia 116 and 7 for 344

FOURTH TEST: 26–30 January (Adelaide)
England won by 106 runs
England 353 and 328
Australia 419 and 156

FIFTH TEST: 3–7 February (Perth)
Australia won by 329 runs
Australia 402 and 8 dec, for 345
England 295 and 123

FACEBOOK MOMENT

Twenty wickets in the first two Tests, illustrated the stronghold
Shane Warne held over England's batsmen.

FOR THE RECORD

Most Runs:	MJ Slater (AUS) 623
Most Wickets:	CJ McDermott (AUS) 32
Highest Score:	MJ Slater (AUS) 176 (First Test)
Best Bowling:	SK Warne (AUS) 8 for 71 (First Test)
Most Catches:	GA Hick (ENG) 9
Highest Run Partnership:	MA Taylor/MJ Slater (AUS) 208 (Third Test, 1st wicket)

Centuries:	**England**	**Australia**
	GF Thorpe	GS Blewett (2)
	MW Gatting	DC Boon
		MJ Slater (3)
		MA Taylor
		ME Waugh

TWITTER FACT

Greg Blewett became the third player after Bill Ponsford and Doug Walters to score Test centuries in their first two Tests.

DID YOU KNOW?

Shane Warne took the first Ashes hat-trick since 1903/04 during the Second Test at the MCG.

1997
IN ENGLAND

ENGLAND	V	AUSTRALIA
MA ATHERTON		MA TAYLOR
WON	DRAWN	WON
2	1	3

England looked like providing that much awaited Ashes comeback when they accounted for Australia in a spirited nine-wicket win at Edgbaston. Australia slumped to 7 for 48 before Shane Warne carried them to 118. In contrast England's reply included Nasser Hussain's career best of 207 and Graham Thorpe's 138. Mark Taylor broke a worrying form slump (he hadn't scored a Test 50 in his previous 21 innings) with 129 while Greg Blewett continued with 125 (the first to score a hundred in his first three Ashes Tests). It wasn't enough as Mike Atherton and Alec Stewart saw England home. A rain-affected draw at Lord's, but not before Glen McGrath's 8 for 38 provided the best figures in 31 Tests there bowling England out for 77. Australia showed its dominance at Old Trafford where Steve Waugh scored two gritty centuries in difficult conditions, Dean Headley who took four wickets in each innings provided the first example of three generations playing Test cricket (after his grandfather George and father Ron played for the West Indies). Ricky Ponting scored his first Ashes ton at Headingley, while Matthew Elliott fell just one short of a double ton, the pair adding 268 for the fifth wicket. The third of the younger trio to star, mullet-haired Jason Gillespie's 7 for 37 returned the best Australian figures in an innings and 61 run victory. England won an amazing match at The Oval after McGrath and Michael Kasprowicz managed seven wickets in each innings. Phil Tufnell's 11 for 93 ensured an England win and the Man of the Match award.

NEWSPAPER HEADLINE

Taylor's Aussies Prevail Again

THE SCOREBOARD

FIRST TEST: 5–8 June (Edgbaston)
England won by 9 wickets
Australia 118 and 447
England 9 dec.for 478 and 1 for 119

SECOND TEST: 19–23 June (Lord's)
Match Drawn
England 77 and 4 for 266
Australia 7 dec. for 213

THIRD TEST: 3–7 July (Old Trafford)
Australia won by 268 runs
Australia 235 and 8 dec. for 395
England 162 and 200

FOURTH TEST: 24–28 July (Headingley)
Australia won by an innings and 61 runs
England 172 and 268
Australia 9 dec. for 501

FIFTH TEST: 7–10 August (Trent Bridge)
Australia won by 264 runs
Australia 427 and 336
England 313 and 186

SIXTH TEST: 21–23 August (The Oval)
England won by 19 runs
England 180 and 163
Australia 220 and 104

FACEBOOK MOMENT

Steve Waugh's twin centuries in a low scoring encounter at Old
Trafford tilted the series back Australia's way and resumed
Australia's dominance with a 268 run win.

FOR THE RECORD

Most Runs:	MTG Elliott (AUS) 556
Most Wickets:	GD McGrath (AUS) 36
Highest Score:	N Hussain (ENG) 207 (First Test)
Best Bowling:	GD McGrath (AUS) 8 for 38 (Second Test)
Most Catches:	GS Blewett (AUS) 9
Highest Run	N Hussain/GP Thorpe (ENG) 288
Partnership:	(First Test, 4th wicket)

Centuries:

England	Australia
N Hussain (2)	GS Blewett
GP Thorpe	MTG Elliott (2)
	RT Ponting
	MA Taylor
	SR Waugh (2)

TWITTER FACT

At Lord's Mike Atherton became England's longest-serving captain
when he led his side for the 42nd time.

DID YOU KNOW?

After a series of injuries Australian all-rounder Shaun Young, who
had been playing for Gloucestershire, was called up into the Aussie
squad and then the Australian side for the Sixth Test at The Oval.
Young scored 0 and 4 not out, bowling just eight economical overs for
the match.

1998–99
IN AUSTRALIA

AUSTRALIA	v	ENGLAND
MA TAYLOR		AJ STEWART
WON	DRAWN	WON
3	1	1

England again struggled to play quality leg spin (despite Warne's shoulder injury) as Stuart's MacGill's 27 wickets at 17 in four Tests show. A thunderstorm in Brisbane with England six wickets down saved the visitors. Steve Waugh, Ian Healy and Michael Slater all scored centuries. Perth's Test was over in two days and two sessions with Jason Gillespie making a memorable comeback taking the final four wickets of the match off six deliveries. The Ashes were decided before Christmas at Adelaide with Justin Langer's undefeated 179 in searing heat, before Glenn McGrath, Damien Fleming, Colin Miller and Stewart MacGill shared the spoils bowling England out for 227. Another hundred from opening batsman Michael Slater set up a total that England had no chance of reaching. The match was overshadowed by the revelation that Warne and Mark Waugh had contacts with Indian bookmakers. A washout of the first day of the Boxing Day Test, didn't stop the most memorable match of the series. Captain and opening batsman, Alec Stewart, unburdened from the gloves, scored a century (107). Mike Atherton made his only Ashes pair as England made only 244 in its second innings. Australia was 2 for 103 before collapsing to 7 for 140, Dean Headley's 6 for 60 helping England home. Australia regained the momentum as MacGill made the most of the turning SCG wicket taking 12 for 107. Darren Gough's hat-trick provided a highlight for England.

NEWSPAPER HEADLINE

MacGill Has England in a Spin

THE SCOREBOARD

FIRST TEST: 20–24 November (Brisbane)
Match Drawn
Australia 485 and 3 dec. for 237
England 375 and 6 for 179

SECOND TEST: 28–30 November (Perth)
Australia won by 7 wickets
England 112 and 191
Australia 240 and 3 for 64

THIRD TEST: 11–15 December (Adelaide)
Australia won by 205 runs
Australia 391 and 5 dec. for 278
England 227 and 237

FOURTH TEST: 26–29 December (Melbourne)
England won by 12 runs
England 270 and 244
Australia 340 and 162

FIFTH TEST: 2–5 January (Sydney)
Australia won by 98 runs
Australia 322 and 184
England 220 and 188

FACEBOOK MOMENT

Jason Gillespie's seven wicket haul at Perth ensured the match was over in two and a half days delivering a killer blow to the England side.

FOR THE RECORD

Most Runs:	SR Waugh (AUS) 498
Most Wickets:	SCG MacGill (AUS) 27
Highest Score:	JL Langer (AUS) 179 not out (Third Test)
Best Bowling:	SCG MacGill (AUS) 7 for 50 (Fifth Test)
Most Catches:	GA Hick (ENG) 11
Highest Run	ME Waugh/SR Waugh (AUS) 190
Partnership:	(Fifth Test, 4th wickets)

Centuries:

England	Australia
MA Butcher	I A Healy
AJ Stewart	JL Langer
	MJ Slater (3)
	ME Waugh
	SR Waugh (2)

TWITTER FACT

Stuart MacGill's 12 for 107, at Sydney were the best figures at the SCG since Charlie Turner in 1888 snared 12 for 87.

DID YOU KNOW?

A new crystal replica of the Ashes urn was presented to Australia for the first time.

CHAPTER 12

THE 2000s

2001
IN ENGLAND

ENGLAND	V	AUSTRALIA
N HUSSAIN (1, 4, 5)		SR WAUGH (1–3, 5)
M ATHERTON (2, 3)		AC GILCHRIST (4)
WON	**DRAWN**	**WON**
1		4

Consecutive victories at Edgbaston, Lord's and Trent Bridge ensured
the Ashes were again safely in Australia's hands. Steve Waugh and
Adam Gilchrist's centuries in the First Test reminded fans of the
veteran's capabilities while Gilchrist provided a sign of things to
come, his 152 included twenty 4s and five 6s. Australia set itself up
for another win at Lord's courtesy of Glenn McGrath's 5 for 54 and
Jason Gillespie's 5 for 53 in the second. Mark Waugh's 108 was the
only century of the match. The Third Test at Nottingham, marked
Mike Atherton's 20th duck creating an England record while pace
bowler Alex Tudor, took 5 for 44 in Australia's first innings. Mark
Butcher's undefeated 173 at Headingley helped England to a win
after Gilchrist set England 311 from 90 overs, a target achieved for
only the second time in Ashes history (the other was at Melbourne in
1928/29). Any chance of an England comeback was snuffed out when
Australia scored 4 for 641 at The Oval including three half centuries.
Justin Langer 102 retired hurt, Mark Waugh 120 and Steve Waugh
an unconquered 157.

NEWSPAPER HEADLINE

Australia's Mental Disintegration of England Continues

THE SCOREBOARD

FIRST TEST: 5–8 July (Edgbaston)
Australia won by an innings and 118 runs.
England 294 and 164
Australia 576

SECOND TEST: 19–22 July (Lord's)
Australia won by 8 wickets
England 187 and 227
Australia 401 and 2 for 14

THIRD TEST: 2–4 August (Trent Bridge)
Australia won by 7 wickets
England 185 and 162
Australia 190 and 3 for 158

FOURTH TEST: 16–20 August (Headingley)
England won by 6 wickets
Australia 447 and 4 for 176
England 309 and 4 for 315

FIFTH TEST: 23–27 August (The Oval)
Australia won by an innings and 25 runs
Australia 4 dec. for 641
England 432 and 184

FACEBOOK MOMENT

Adam Gilchrist's 152, his first Ashes hundred, including 22 runs off a Mark Butcher over, equalled the most expensive over in Ashes history. And set the scene for Australia's dominance.

FOR THE RECORD

Most Runs:	MA Butcher (ENG) 456
Most Wickets:	GD McGrath (AUS) 32
Highest Score:	MA Butcher (ENG) 173 not out (Fifth Test)
Best Bowling:	GD McGrath (AUS) 7 for 76 (Second Test)
Most Catches:	ME Waugh (AUS) 9
Highest Run Partnership:	RT Ponting/ME Waugh (AUS) 221 (Fourth Test, 3rd wicket)

Centuries:

England	**Australia**
MA Butcher	AC Gilchrist
MR Ramprakash	JL Langer
	DR Martyn (2)
	RT Ponting
	ME Waugh (2)
	SE Waugh (2)

TWITTER FACT

England captain Mike Atherton retired from Test cricket after the Fifth Test at The Oval.

DID YOU KNOW?

The Waugh brothers echoed the performance of Ian and Greg Chappell, scoring centuries in the final innings of the Fifth Test at The Oval, 26 years later.

2002–03
IN AUSTRALIA

AUSTRALIA	V	ENGLAND
SR WAUGH		N HUSSAIN
WON	DRAWN	WON
4		1

England never really recovered after Nasser Hussain put Australia in to bat at Brisbane only to watch the home team finish the day at 2 for 364. Matt Hayden's century in each innings and Ricky Ponting's 123 made England's bowlers resemble a pea shooter attack. England's second innings 79 highlighted the chasm between the sides. Australia continued its dominance with innings wins in Adelaide and Perth, despite Michael Vaughan's 177 in the Second Test. England's opening efforts meant little when they subsequently lost 6 for 47. Australia began the Boxing Day Test hammering England's bowlers with Hayden (102) and Justin Langer (250) rejoicing in the batting display. On the final day England's bowlers made something of a comeback with Steve Harmison and Andrew Caddick making Australia sweat reaching the required 107 runs. England continued its improving form winning the final Test at Sydney, by 225 runs. Vaughan again showed his international class with his 183, while Caddick's ten wickets for the match provided the highlight of his career. Steve Waugh ended a summer of indifferent form with his 29th Test century and also passed the 10,000 Test run mark.

NEWSPAPER HEADLINE

England Lose but Show Signs of Recovery

THE SCOREBOARD

FIRST TEST: 7–11 November (Brisbane)

Australia won by 384 runs

Australia 492

England 325 and 79

SECOND TEST: 21–25 November (Adelaide)

Australia won by an innings and 51 runs

England 324 and 159

Australia 9 dec. for 552

THIRD TEST: 29 November–3 December (Perth)

Australia won by an innings and 48 runs

England 185 and 223

Australia 456

FOURTH TEST: 26–30 December (Melbourne)

Australia won by 5 wickets

Australia 6 dec. for 551 and 5 for 107

England 270 and 387

FIFTH TEST: 2–6 January (Sydney)

England won by 225 runs

England 362 and 9 dec. for 452

Australia 363 and 226

FACEBOOK MOMENT

When England captain Nasser Hussain sent Australia into bat in the First Test at Brisbane and the home team made 492 (despite four batsmen failing to score) any potential psychological advantage was lost. When England's strike bowler Simon Jones, badly injured his right knee the news only worsened for England.

FOR THE RECORD

Most Runs:	MP Vaughan (ENG) 633
Most Wickets:	JN Gillespie (AUS), AR Caddick (ENG) 20
Highest Score:	JL Langer (AUS) 250 (Fourth Test)
Best Bowling:	AR Caddick (ENG) 7 for 94 (Fifth Test)
Most Catches:	ML Hayden (AUS) 8
Highest Run Partnership:	ML Hayden/RT Ponting (AUS) 243 (First Test, 2nd wicket)

Centuries:

England	Australia
MA Butcher	AC Gilchrist
MP Vaughan (3)	ML Hayden (3)
	JL Langer
	RT Ponting (2)
	SR Waugh

TWITTER FACT

Australia went into a Test match for the first time in 12 years without Glenn McGrath and Shane Warne in the final Test at Sydney and lost by 225 runs.

DID YOU KNOW?

Steve Waugh's century off the final ball of the second day in the Fifth Test at the SCG was a fitting Ashes finale. It was Waugh's 29th ton as he also equalled Allan Border's 156 Test match appearances.

2005
IN ENGLAND

ENGLAND	V	AUSTRALIA
MP VAUGHAN		RT PONTING
WON	DRAWN	WON
2	2	1

Finally, after eight series losses, England bounced back to win the Ashes at home. Before the first ball was bowled, it was clear England was stronger having lost only one of its previous 14 Tests. Australia repeated its Lord's form but not before Steve Harmison's aggressive bowling had the visitors all out for 190. Glenn McGrath produced a devastating bowling display, taking 5 for 2 in 31 balls, while newcomer Kevin Pietersen made two half centuries. At Edgbaston, a rejuvenated home side produced one of the most thrilling wins in Test history. McGrath was injured in a practice session before play, but it was Andrew Flintoff's scintillating 141 runs and seven wickets in the Test which provided the counterbalance to Warne's match figures of 10 for 162.

Australia recovered from 7 for 137 to come to within three runs of victory before Geraint Jones took the leg side catch off Michael Kasprowicz to win the match. Old Trafford marked a classic 166 from Michael Vaughan while Simon Jones 6 for 53, helped England gain control. Ricky Ponting's 156 in almost 7 hours staved off defeat. England's 477 at Trent Bridge and its rolling of Australia for 218 made Australia follow-on for the first time in two decades of Ashes contests. Although Jones' loss damaged England's bowling stocks their batting also let them down as the home side collapsed to 7 for 116. Ashley Giles and Matthew Hoggard eventually helped England to a win. The Oval Test saw Andrew Strauss make his second ton of the series while Australian opener Matthew Hayden returned to form with a century as did fellow opener Justin Langer.

Despite Warne dropping Pietersen on 15 the England star scored 158 (considered one of the great Ashes knocks of all time) and ensured a draw. England had won the series after 16 years and 42 days.

NEWSPAPER HEADLINE

England Reign Again After 16 Years!

THE SCOREBOARD

FIRST TEST: 21 July –25 July (Lord's)
Australia won by 239 runs
Australia 190 and 384
England 155 and 180

SECOND TEST: 4–7 August (Edgbaston)
England won by 2 runs * Ashes record
England 407 and 182
Australia 308 and 279

THIRD TEST: 11–15 August (Old Trafford)
Match Drawn
England 444 and 5 for 115
Australia 302 and 9 for 371

FOURTH TEST: 25–28 August (Trent Bridge)
England won by 3 wickets
England 477 and 7 for 129
Australia 218 and 387

FIFTH TEST: 8–12 September (The Oval)
Match Drawn
England 373 and 335
Australia 367 and 0 for 4

FACEBOOK MOMENT

When England wicketkeeper Geraint Jones, caught a Michael Kasprowicz gloved ball down the leg side England had levelled the series. Had England been down 0–2, it would have been over.

FOR THE RECORD

Most Runs: KP Pietersen (ENG) 473
Most Wickets: SK Warne (AUS) 40
Highest Score: MP Vaughan (ENG) 166 (Third Test)
Best Bowling: SK Warne (ENG) 6 for 46 (Second Test)
Most Catches: ML Hayden (AUS) 10
Highest Run JL Langer/M Hayden (AUS) 185
Partnership: (Fifth Test, 1st wicket)
Centuries:

England	Australia
A Flintoff	JL Langer
KP Pietersen	ML Hayden
AJ Strauss (2)	RT Ponting
MP Vaughan	

TWITTER FACT

England used only 12 players for the entire series, the only line-up change coming after an injury to Simon Jones saw Paul Collingwood come in for the last Test and earn him an MBE.

DID YOU KNOW?

'Jerusalem', England's unofficial anthem for the series, was released as a single and made the UK Top 20 music charts.

2006–07
IN AUSTRALIA

AUSTRALIA	v	ENGLAND
RT PONTING		A FLINTOFF
WON	DRAWN	WON
5		0

After more than 14 months of anticipation Steve Harmison's opening delivery that ended up in the hands of second slip provided an embarrassment for the visitors and a psychological advantage to the Australians. The home side' first innings 9 declared for 602 featured a scintillating 196 from the Ricky Ponting, while Glenn McGrath's 6 for 50 set up an easy win. In Adelaide, Collingwood scored a valiant 206 combining with Kevin Pietersen (158) as England scored 6 for 551 in its first innings. A draw looked most likely as Ricky Ponting and Michael Clarke helped Australia to 513, while Matthew Hoggard's 7 for 109 echoed some of his 2005 form. Despite a lead of 97, Warne's 4 for 49 in England's second innings led to a six-wicket win. England looked in the game in Perth bowling Australia out for 244 with left-arm orthodox spinner Monty Panesar's 5 for 92 illustrating his under use. The visitors again failed to gain any advantage by replying with 215. Adam Gilchrist smashed the second fastest ton in Test history as Australia made another 500 plus score. The Alistair Cook and Ian Bell's 170 run partnership in England's second innings wasn't enough, the visitors tallied up another loss, this time by 206 runs. The route continued at the MCG this time by an innings and 99 runs. A Boxing Day crowd of 89,155 saw Warne power through England with 5 for 39 as they collapsed to 159. Australia stumbled initially in reply losing 5 for 84, before being rescued by Matthew Hayden and Andrew Symonds scoring his debut Test ton. Sydney proved a spinners paradise with Warne and McGill taking 17 of the 20 wickets to fall, England suffered to a ten wicket loss to complete a 5–0 whitewash.

NEWSPAPER HEADLINE

Australia's 5–0 Ashes Whitewash

THE SCOREBOARD

FIRST TEST: 23–27 Nov (Brisbane)

Australia won by 277 runs

Australia 9 for 603 and 1 dec. for 202

England 157 and 370

SECOND TEST: 1–5 December (Adelaide)

Australia won 6 wickets

England 6 dec. for 551 and 129

Australia 513 and 4 for 168

THIRD TEST: 14–18 December (Perth)

Australia won by 206 runs

Australia 244 and 5 dec. for 527

England 215 and 350

FOURTH TEST: 26–29 December (Melbourne)

Australia won by an innings and 99 runs

England 159 and 161

Australia 419

FIFTH TEST: 2–5 January (Sydney)

Australia won by 10 wickets

England 291 and 147

Australia 393 and 0 for 46

FACEBOOK MOMENT

England Steve Harmison's opening delivery that was so wide it ended up in the hands of second slip proved one of the great anticlimaxes in Ashes history and provided an early psychological advantage to the Australians.

FOR THE RECORD

Most Runs: RT Ponting (AUS) 576
Most Wickets: SR Clark (ENG) 26
Highest Score: PD Collingwood (ENG) 206 (Second Test)
Best Bowling: MJ Hoggard (ENG) 7 for 109 (Second Test)
Most Catches: PD Collingwood (ENG), ML Hayden (AUS) 7
Highest Run PD Collingwood/KP Pietersen (ENG) 310
Partnership: (Second Test, 4th wicket)

Centuries:	**England**	**Australia**
	AN Cook	MJ Clarke (2)
	PD Collingwood	AC Gilchrist
	KP Pietersen	ML Hayden
		MEK Hussey
		JL Langer
		RT Ponting (2)
		A Symonds

TWITTER FACT

Overlooked for Test matches in Australia's losing 2005 series, Mike Hussey scored 458 runs, finishing with an average of 91 in 2006–07, his first Ashes series.

DID YOU KNOW?

Before we knew the effect that Twenty-20 cricket would have cricket more than 17,000 fans watched an Ashes legends game won by England by 7 wickets.

2009
IN ENGLAND

ENGLAND	V	AUSTRALIA
AJ STRAUSS		RT PONTING
WON	DRAWN	WON
2	2	1

High scoring dominated the first innings for both sides in the First Test at Cardiff. England's 435 featured three half centuries while Australia's 6 declared for 674 put the match out of reach. Paul Collingwood batted for almost six hours for 74, while James Anderson and Monty Panesar held out as the home side limped to 9 for 252. Andrew Strauss and Alastair Cook's opening stand of 196 set England up for a much bigger total than the 425 it achieved. Anderson's four wickets saw Australia lose 6 for 69 in its first innings while Andrew Flintoff took five in the second creating an England Ashes win at Lord's for the first time in 75 years. At Edgbaston, Anderson again with five wickets and Graham Onions four reduced Australia to 263 after losing 7 for 77. Clarke and Marcus North's 185 runs partnership brought a renewed sense of confidence during the drawn match. Australia's only win of the series at Headingley was precipitated by Peter Siddle's 5 for 21, as England crumbled to 102. Australia's 445 from 104 overs helped by a North century overwhelmed the home side as England were again bowled out cheaply for 263. Ben Hilfenhaus continued his good form with four wickets, while the much-maligned Mitchell Johnson took five. At The Oval, Stuart Broad and Graeme Swann helped bowl out Australia for 160 providing England with a first innings lead. Jonathan Trott's debut century helped set Australia 546 for victory. At 2 for 217, this looked possible until two clever pieces of fielding by Flintoff and then Strauss saw Ponting and Clarke both run out within 5 balls and the end of Australia's chances of winning the series.

NEWSPAPER HEADLINE

Ignore the Stats ... England's Ashes!

THE SCOREBOARD

FIRST TEST: 8–12 July (Cardiff)
Match Drawn
England 435 and 9 for 252
Australia 6 dec. for 674

SECOND TEST: 16 July–20 July (Lord's)
England won by 115 runs
England 425 and 6 dec. for 311
Australia 215 and 406

THIRD TEST: 30 July– 3 August (Edgbaston)
Match Drawn
Australia 263 and 5 for 375
England 376

FOURTH TEST: 7–9 August (Headingley)
Australia won by an innings and 80 runs
England 102 and 263
Australia 445

FIFTH TEST: 20–23 August (The Oval)
England won by 197 runs
England 332 and 9 dec. for 373
Australia 160 and 348

FACEBOOK MOMENT

Andrew Strauss and Alastair Cook's opening stand of 196 helped set
up England's first Ashes win at Lord's for 75 years.

FOR THE RECORD

Most Runs:	AJ Strauss (ENG) 474
Most Wickets:	BW Hilfenhaus (AUS) 22
Highest Score:	AJ Strauss (ENG) 161 (Second Test)
Best Bowling:	SCJ Broad (ENG) 6 for 91 (Fourth Test)
Most Catches:	RT Ponting (AUS) 11
Highest Run Partnership:	SM Katich/RT Ponting (AUS) 239 (First Test, 2nd wicket)

Centuries:

England	Australia
AJ Strauss	MJ Clarke (2)
IJL Trott	BJ Haddin
	MEK Hussey
	SM Katich
	MJ North (2)
	RT Ponting

TWITTER FACT

Australia had the better of the statistics but lost the series.

DID YOU KNOW?

Australia's batsmen scored eight centuries to England's two. The visitors even had three bowlers who took at least 20 wickets (Hilfenhaus, Siddle and Johnson) but Ricky Ponting later acknowledged that England won because they took wickets and made runs 'at the right times'.

SYDNEY CRICKET GROUND, 2000s

2010–11
IN AUSTRALIA

AUSTRALIA	V	ENGLAND
RT PONTING (1–4) MJ CLARKE (5)		A STRAUSS
WON	DRAWN	WON
1	1	3

This time the statistics reflected the final outcome of the series. A drawn opener at Brisbane included Australia's Peter Siddle's hat-trick (Alastair Cook, Matt Prior and Stuart Broad). Australia responded to England's 260 with the help of Michael Hussey's 195 and Brad Haddin's 136 adding 307 for the sixth wicket. England's extraordinary 1 for 517, included Andrew Strauss narrowly missing registering a pair, later making his way to 110, while Cook's undefeated 235 helped add 329 with Jonathan Trott's 135 not out. Adelaide hosted the Second Test where Australia lost its first three wickets in 2.1 overs. Cook, with 148 and Kevin Pietersen, 227 led the response as England accumulated 5 declared for 620. Graeme Swann's 5 for 91 helped dismiss Australia for 304, despite Michael Clarke's 80. Australia fought back at Perth after Mitchell Johnson's 6 for 38 and Ryan Harris' 6 for 47 providing an indication of their abilities. Hussey was the only centurion of the low scoring Test with 116 while Chris Tremlett's 5 for 87 stood out for the England attack. In Melbourne Australia collapsed to 98 while an opening stand of 168 from Strauss and Cook helped England to 513. Despite Haddin's undefeated 55, Australia capitulated for 258, leading to an innings loss by the fourth morning. In Sydney, the visitors recovered from 5 for 226 to post 644 after Australia had limped to 280. England's massive total included four centuries (Cook, Strauss, Bell and Prior).

NEWSPAPER HEADLINE

England's Turn To Dominate

THE SCOREBOARD

FIRST TEST: 25–29 November (Brisbane)
Drawn Match
England 260 and 1 dec. for 517
Australia 481 and 1 for 107.

SECOND TEST: 3–7 December (Adelaide)
England won by an innings and 71 runs
Australia 245 and 304
England 5 dec. for 620

THIRD TEST: 16–20 December (Perth)
Australia won by 267 runs
Australia 268 and 309
England 187 and 123

FOURTH TEST: 26–30 December (Melbourne)
England won by an innings and 157 runs
Australia 98 and 258
England 513

FIFTH TEST: 3–7 January
England won by an innings and 83 runs
Australia 280 and 281
England 644

FACEBOOK MOMENT

When Australia collapsed to be bowled out for 98 on the first day of the Boxing Day Test in front of 84,345 at the MCG, it was Australia's lowest first innings in a home Ashes Test since 1936.

FOR THE RECORD

Most Runs:	AN Cook (ENG) 766
Most Wickets:	JM Anderson (ENG) 24
Highest Score:	AN Cook (ENG) 235 not out (First Test)
Best Bowling:	MG Johnson (AUS) 6 for 38 (Third Test)
Most Catches:	PD Collingwood (ENG) 9
Highest Run	AN Cook/IJL Trott (ENG) 329
Partnership:	(First Test, 2nd wicket)

Centuries:

England	**Australia**
IR Bell	BJ Haddin
AN Cook (3)	MEK Hussey (2)
KP Pietersen	
M Prior	
AJ Strauss	
IJL Trott (2)	

TWITTER FACT

England star Kevin Pietersen's 227 in the Second Test was his highest score in Test cricket.

DID YOU KNOW?

Once arguably the best batsman in the world, Ricky Ponting averaged just 16 throughout the series, the lowest from an Aussie skipper in an Ashes series for 50 years.

2013
IN ENGLAND

ENGLAND	V	AUSTRALIA
AN COOK		MJ CLARKE
WON	DRAWN	WON
3	2	0

An enthralling series opener saw England win the First Test of a series for the first time since 1997. Peter's Siddle's 5 for 50 set the scene for the much-maligned Aussies who had switched coaches just days before the Ashes began. Australia looked to be squandering that opportunity until Phillip Hughes and Test debutante Ashton Agar added 163 creating the highest tenth wicket partnership in Test history. An Ian Bell century set Australia 311 to win, but they fell short by 15 runs in the afternoon session of the fifth day. Lord's marked another home side victory, but this time in more emphatic fashion. Bell became the fourth Englishman to score three figures in three consecutive Tests. Joe Root's second innings 180 and Graeme Swann's nine wickets for the match completed the rout for England. At Old Trafford England's bowlers could do little to blunt the effectiveness of Michael Clarke, as Australia waltzed to 7 declared for 527. Pietersen responded with 113 and England 368. Rain and bad light on day four reduced play to 56 overs while only 20 overs could be bowled on the final day. Another relatively low scoring encounter at Chester-le-Street saw England claim an unassailable 3–0 lead. Ian Bell scored his third century of the series and Australian Chris Rogers his first. Stuart Broad's 11 wickets for the match ensuring Australia did not reach 300 in either innings. Australia's 9 for 492 at The Oval set England up for a thrilling final day chase of 227 from 44 overs where they fell just 21 runs short when the umpires called 'bad light' with four overs remaining.

NEWSPAPER HEADLINE

Back-to-Back Ashes for England!

THE SCOREBOARD

FIRST TEST: 10–14 July (Trent Bridge)
England won by 14 runs
England 215 and 375
Australia 280 and 296

SECOND TEST: 18–21 July (Lord's)
England won by 347 runs
England 361 and 7 dec. for 349
Australia 128 and 235

THIRD TEST: 1–5 August (Old Trafford)
Match Drawn
Australia 7 dec. for 527 and 7 dec. for 172
England 368 and 3 for 37

FOURTH TEST: 9–12 August (Chester-le-street)
England won by 74 runs
England 238 and 330
Australia 270 and 224

FIFTH TEST: 21–25 August (The Oval)
Match Drawn
Australia 9 for 492 and 6 dec. for 111
England 377 and 5 for 206

FACEBOOK MOMENT

England bowled Australia out just 14 runs short of the target in the
First Test at Trent Bridge proving the home side were still able to win
when Australia bowled at its best.

FOR THE RECORD

Most Runs:	IR Bell (ENG) 562
Most Wickets:	GP Swann (ENG) 26
Highest Score:	JE Root (ENG) 180 (Second Test)
Best Bowling:	RJ Harris (AUS) 7 for 117 (Fourth Test)
Most Catches:	AN Cook (ENG) 7
Highest Run Partnership:	MJ Clarke/SPD Smith (AUS) 214 (Third Test, 4th wicket)

Centuries:

England	Australia
IR Bell (3)	MJ Clarke
KP Pietersen	CL Rogers
JE Root	SPD Smith
IJL Trott	SR Watson

TWITTER FACT

Ashton Agar's 98 at Trent Bridge created a record for the highest score for a number 11 and for a player in his Test debut.

DID YOU KNOW?

447 runs were scored on the final day of the Fifth Test at The Oval, creating a record for an Ashes contest.

2013–14
IN AUSTRALIA

AUSTRALIA	V	ENGLAND
MJ CLARKE		AN COOK
WON	DRAWN	WON
5		0

Australia's reduction to 6 for 132 meant little at the opening Test at the Gabba. Haddin (94) took the home side to 295 before the Mitchell Johnson blitzkrieg began as England succumbed to 136. David's Warner's second innings 124 and Michael Clarke's 113 helped Australia exceed the 400 run mark. Kevin Pietersen's 100th Test ended with dual failures as Johnson took his match tally to nine wickets. Australia romped to 9 declared for 570 while Johnson's annihilation of England continued bowling the tourists out for 172; Ian Bell's undefeated 72, the only signs of England resistance. By the time Peter Siddle helped bowl England out for 312, Australia was 2–nil in the series. More was to follow at the WACA where Australia regained the Ashes after centuries to Steve Smith (111) and Warner 112. In just his second Test, Ben Stokes managed 120 as Johnson again tore through the England line-up. A record crowd of 91,092 watched England drearily make it to 6 for 226 by stumps. Pietersen continued to be one of his side's key performers with 71 despite the rumours of the turmoil within England ranks. England's 255 proved the highest total of the match although Australia's second innings run chase of 2 for 231 with Chris Rogers' 116 showed what could be achieved on the MCG pitch. Australia's 5–0 sweep of the series continued at Sydney as England was bowled out for 155 and 166. Tons to Smith and Rogers while Stoke's first innings 6 for 99 reinforced the talented young all-rounder's promotion to Test level.

NEWSPAPER HEADLINE

England Blown Away

THE SCOREBOARD

FIRST TEST: 21–25 November (Brisbane)
Australia won by 381 runs
Australia 295 and 7 dec. for 401
England 136 and 179

SECOND TEST: 5–9 December (Adelaide)
Australia won by 218 runs
Australia 9 dec. for 570 and 3 dec. for 132
England 172 and 312

THIRD TEST: 13–17 December (Perth)
Australia won by 150 runs
Australia 385 and 6 dec. for 369
England 251 and 353

FOURTH TEST: 26–30 December (Melbourne)
Australia won by 8 wickets
England 255 and 179
Australia 204 and 2 for 231

FIFTH TEST: 3–7 January (Sydney)
Australia won by 281 runs
Australia 326 and 276
England 155 and 166

FACEBOOK MOMENT

Mitchell's Johnson's pace bowling revived memories of what Dennis Lillee and Jeff Thomson did to England in 1974/75.

FOR THE RECORD

Most Runs:	DA Warner (AUS) 523
Most Wickets:	MJ Johnson (AUS) 37
Highest Score:	MJ Clarke (AUS) 148 (Second Test)
Best Bowling:	MJ Johnson (AUS) 7 for 40 (Second Test)
Most Catches:	GJ Bailey (AUS) 10
Highest Run Partnership:	MJ Clarke/BJ Haddin (AUS) 200 (Second Test, 6th wicket)

Centuries:	**England**	**Australia**
	BA Stokes	MJ Clarke (2)
		BJ Haddin
		CL Rogers (2)
		SPD Smith (2)
		DA Warner (2)
		SR Watson

TWITTER FACT

A stress-related illness caused England's number three batsman Jonathan Trott, who had excelled against Australia in the preceding series, to withdraw after the First Test.

DID YOU KNOW?

The Boxing Day crowd of 91,092 broke the Australia attendance record that had stood since the 1960/61 West Indies tour.

2015
IN ENGLAND

ENGLAND	V	AUSTRALIA
AN COOK		MJ CLARKE
WON	DRAWN	WON
3	0	2

Although the score line suggest a more even contest, England held the upper hand throughout the series. Ian Bell stepped up when required, emerging talent Joe Root reinforced his growing reputation as the only batsman to score two centuries in the series. Australian opener Chris Rogers proved he could perform consistently at Test level in England drawing a close to a fine, short and belated Test career. England rarely looked back after its opening series score of 430. Root, with 134, again provided stability in England's second innings when they wobbled. Australia levelled the series at their favourite of all English hunting grounds, Lord's, after Steve Smith's 215. The visitors showed a sign of what was to come lasting 36.4 overs in the first innings at Edgbaston, making just 136. Steve Finn's 6 for 79 put the nail in Australia's coffin for the match. Bell's steadying hand again vital to England's successful run chase. Stuart Broad surprised everyone, including himself, in bowling Australia out for 60 at Trent Bridge. Joe Root managed to more than double Australia's score with his own bat (130). Ben Stokes added to the visitors' woes with 6 for 36 as they succumbed to 253, despite Warner's resistant 64. With the series over, Steve Smith's 143 set Australia up for an innings and 46 run victory at The Oval.

Joe Root Steps Up for England

THE SCOREBOARD

FIRST TEST: 8–11 July (Cardiff)

England won by 169 runs

England 430 and 289

Australia 308 and 242

SECOND TEST: 16–19 July (Lord's)

Australia won by 405 runs

Australia 8 dec. for 566 and 2 dec. for 254

England 312 and 103

THIRD TEST: 29 July– 31 July (Edgbaston)

England won by 8 wickets

Australia 136 and 265

England 281 and 2 for 242

FOURTH TEST: 6–8 August (Trent Bridge)

England won by an innings and 78 runs

Australia 60 and 253

England 9 dec. for 391

FIFTH TEST: 20–23 August (The Oval)

Australia won by an innings and 46 runs

Australia 481

England 149 and 286

FACEBOOK MOMENT

With England 2–1 and with two matches to play Stuart Broad's 8 for 15 at Trent Bridge to bowl Australia out for 60 ended any hope for the visitors.

FOR THE RECORD

Most Runs:	SPD Smith (AUS) 508	
Most Wickets:	SCJ Broad (ENG) 21	
Highest Score:	SPD Smith (AUS) 215 (Second Test)	
Best Bowling:	SCJ Broad (ENG) 8 for 15 (Fourth Test)	
Most Catches:	AN Cook (ENG) 9	
Highest Run	CLJ Rogers/SPD Smith (AUS) 284	
Partnership:	(Second Test, 2nd wicket)	
Centuries:	**England**	**Australia**
	JE Root (2)	CLR Rogers
		SPD Smith (2)

TWITTER FACT

Ian Bell joined Ian Botham as just the second player to play in five Ashes winnings series.

DID YOU KNOW?

Extras top scored for Australia in the first innings of the Fourth Test with 14.

2017–18
IN AUSTRALIA

ENGLAND	V	AUSTRALIA
WON	DRAWN	WON

NEWSPAPER HEADLINE

THE SCOREBOARD

First Test:

Second Test:

Third Test:

Fourth Test:

Fifth Test:

FACEBOOK MOMENT

FOR THE RECORD

Most Runs:

Most Wickets:

Highest Score:

Best Bowling:

Most Catches:

Highest Run
Partnership:

Centuries: England   Australia

APPENDIX

RESULTS

1882–2015*

(*not including 2017 Ashes series)

SERIES

Team	Series	Won	Lost	Tied	Drawn
Australia	69	32	32	0	5
England	69	32	32	0	5

AT HOME

Team	Series	Won	Lost	Tied	Draw
Australia	34	18	14	0	2
England	35	19	13	0	3

MATCHES

Team	Tests	Won	Lost	Tied	Draw
Australia	325	130	106	0	89
England	325	106	130	0	89

AT HOME

Team	Tests	Won	Lost	Tied	Draw
Australia	162	82	56	0	25
England	163	50	48	0	64

DRAWN ASHES SERIES

Series 29.	1938 in England (Australia retained Ashes)
Series 41.	1962–63 in Australia (Australia retained Ashes)
Series 43.	1965–66 in Australia (Australia retained Ashes)
Series 45.	1968 in England (Australia retained Ashes)
Series 46.	1972 in England (England retained Ashes)

SERIES IN AUSTRALIA

Series 1.	1882–83 in Australia	2–1 (3)	
Series 3.	1884–85 in Australia	3–2 (5)	
Series 5.	1886–87 in Australia	2–0 (2)	
Series 6.	1887–88 in Australia	1–0 (1)	
Series 9.	1891–92 in Australia	2–1 (3)	*
Series 11.	1894–95 in Australia	3–2 (5)	
Series 13.	1897–98 in Australia	4–1 (5)	*
Series 15.	1901–02 in Australia	4–1 (5)	* R
Series 17.	1903–04 in Australia	3–2 (5)	
Series 19.	1907–08 in Australia	2–0 (5)	*
Series 21.	1911–12 in Australia	4–1 (5)	
Series 23.	1920–21 in Australia	5–0 (5)	*
Series 25.	1924–25 in Australia	4–1 (5)	*
Series 27.	1928–29 in Australia	4–1 (5)	
Series 29.	1932–33 in Australia	4–1 (5)	
Series 31.	1936–37 in Australia	3–2 (5)	* R
Series 33.	1946–47 in Australia	3–0 (5)	* R
Series 35.	1950–51 in Australia	4–1 (5)	* R
Series 37.	1954–55 in Australia	3–1 (5)	
Series 39.	1958–59 in Australia	4–0 (5)	*
Series 41.	1962–63 in Australia	1–1 (5)	* (D) R
Series 43.	1965–66 in Australia	1–1 (5)	* (D) R
Series 45.	1970–71 in Australia	2–0 (7)	
Series 47.	1974–75 in Australia	4–1 (6)	*
Series 50.	1978–79 in Australia	5–1 (6)	
Series 52.	1982–83 in Australia	2–1 (5)	*
Series 54.	1986–87 in Australia	2–1 (5)	
Series 56.	1990–91 in Australia	3–0 (5)	* R
Series 58.	1994–95 in Australia	3–1 (5)	* R
Series 60.	1998–99 in Australia	3–1 (5)	* R
Series 62.	2002–03 in Australia	4–1 (5)	* R
Series 64.	2006–07 in Australia	2–1 (5)	*
Series 66.	2010–11 in Australia	3–1 (5)	
Series 68.	2013–14 in Australia	5–0 (5)	*
Series 70.	2017–18 in Australia (35th home series)		

KEY: * won on home soil   R retained Ashes   (D) drawn series

SERIES IN ENGLAND

Series 2.	1884 in England	1–0 (3)	*
Series 4.	1886 in England	3–0 (3)	* R
Series 7.	1888 in England	2–1 (3)	*
Series 8.	1890 in England	2–0 (2)	*
Series 10.	1893 in England	1–0 (3)	* R
Series 12.	1896 in England	2–1 (3)	* R
Series 14.	1899 in England	1–0 (5)	
Series 16.	1902 in England	2–1 (5)	
Series 18.	1905 in England	4–1 (5)	* R
Series 20.	1909 in England	2–1 (5)	*
Series 22.	1912 in England	1–0 (3)	* R
Series 24.	1921 in England	3–0 (5)	
Series 26.	1926 in England	1–0 (5)	*
Series 28.	1930 in England	2–1 (5)	
Series 30.	1934 in England	2–1 (5)	
Series 32.	1938 in England	1–1 (4)	(D)
Series 34.	1948 in England	4–0 (5)	
Series 36.	1953 in England	1–0 (5)	*
Series 38.	1956 in England	2–1 (5)	* R
Series 40.	1961 in England	2–1 (5)	
Series 42.	1964 in England	1–0 (5)	
Series 44.	1968 in England	1–1 (5)	(D)
Series 46.	1972 in England	2–2 (5)	(D) R
Series 48.	1975 in England	1–0 (4)	
Series 49.	1977 in England	3–0 (5)	*
Series 51.	1981 in England	3–1 (6)	* R
Series 53.	1985 in England	3–1 (6)	* R
Series 55.	1989 in England	4–0 (6)	
Series 57.	1993 in England	4–1 (6)	
Series 59.	1997 in England	3–2 (6)	
Series 61.	2001 in England	4–1 (5)	
Series 63.	2005 in England	5–0 (5)	*
Series 65.	2009 in England	2–1 (5)	*
Series 67.	2013 in England	3–0 (5)	* R
Series 69.	2015 in England	3–2 (5)	*

KEY: * won on home soil   R retained Ashes   (D) drawn series

MOST ASHES MATCHES

PLAYER	CAREER	M	RUNS	HS	AVE
SE Gregory (AUS)	1890–1912	52	2193	201	25.80
SR Waugh (AUS)	1986–2003	45	3173	177*	58.75
MC Cowdrey (ENG)	1954–1975	43	2433	113	34.26
WW Armstrong (AUS)	1902–1921	42	2172	158	35.03
AR Border (AUS)	1978–1993	42	3222	200*	55.55
C Hill (AUS)	1896–1912	41	2660	188	35.46
JB Hobbs (ENG)	1908–1930	41	3636	187	54.26
W Rhodes (ENG)	1899–1926	41	1706	179	31.01
VT Trumper (AUS)	1899–1912	40	2263	185*	32.79
GA Gooch (ENG)	1975–1995	39	2436	196	33.36
MA Noble (AUS)	1898–1909	39	1905	133	30.72
DI Gower (ENG)	1978–1991	38	3037	215	46.01
WAS Oldfield (AUS)	1920–1937	38	1116	65*	23.25
DG Bradman (AUS)	1928–1948	37	5028	334	89.78
RN Harvey (AUS)	1948–1963	37	2416	167	38.34
RW Marsh (AUS)	1970–1983	37	1409	92*	25.61

MOST ASHES RUNS

PLAYER	CAREER	MAT	INNS	RUNS	HS	AVE	100S
DG Bradman (AUS)	1928–1948	37	63	5028	334	89.78	19
JB Hobbs (ENG)	1908–1930	41	71	3636	187	54.26	12
AR Border (AUS)	1978–1993	42	73	3222	200*	55.55	7
SR Waugh (AUS)	1986–2003	45	72	3173	177*	58.75	10
DI Gower (ENG)	1978–1991	38	69	3037	215	46.01	9
WR Hammond (ENG)	1928–1947	33	58	2852	251	51.85	9
H Sutcliffe (ENG)	1924–1934	27	46	2741	194	66.85	8
C Hill (AUS)	1896–1912	41	76	2660	188	35.46	4
JH Edrich (ENG)	1964–1975	32	57	2644	175	48.96	7
G Boycott (ENG)	1964–1981	34	63	2579	191	46.05	6
MA Taylor (AUS)	1989–1999	33	61	2496	219	42.30	6
RT Ponting (AUS)	1997–2010	35	58	2476	196	44.21	8
GA Gooch (ENG)	1975–1995	39	73	2436	196	33.36	4
MC Cowdrey (ENG)	1954–1975	43	75	2433	113	34.26	5
L Hutton (ENG)	1938–1955	27	49	2428	364	56.46	5

KEY: * not out

MOST ASHES MATCHES AS CAPTAIN

PLAYER	CAREER	M	W	L	D	W%
AR Border (AUS)	1985–1993	28	13	6	9	46.42
AC MacLaren (ENG)	1897–1909	22	4	11	7	18.18
DG Bradman (AUS)	1936–1948	19	11	3	5	57.89
RT Ponting (AUS)	2005–2010	19	8	6	5	42.10
J Darling (AUS)	1899–1905	18	5	4	9	27.77
IM Chappell (AUS)	1971–1975	16	7	4	5	43.75
MJ Clarke (AUS)	2011–2015	16	7	7	2	43.75
MA Taylor (AUS)	1994–1999	16	9	4	3	56.25
MA Atherton (ENG)	1993–2001	15	4	9	2	26.66
JM Brearley (ENG)	1977–1981	15	11	1	3	73.33
AN Cook (ENG)	2013–2015	15	6	7	2	40.00
MA Noble (AUS)	1903–1909	15	8	5	2	53.33
WM Woodfull (AUS)	1930–1934	15	5	6	4	33.33
R Benaud (AUS)	1958–1963	14	6	2	6	42.85
WG Grace (ENG)	1888–1899	13	8	3	2	61.53

MOST ASHES DISMISSALS

WICKETKEEPER	CAREER	MAT	INNS	DIS
IA Healy (AUS)	1989–1999	33	65	135
RW Marsh (AUS)	1970–1983	37	72	131
APE Knott (ENG)	1968–1981	33	64	101
AC Gilchrist (AUS)	2001–2007	20	40	96
WAS Oldfield (AUS)	1920–1937	38	69	90
AFA Lilley (ENG)	1896–1909	32	61	84
BJ Haddin (AUS)	2009–2015	20	37	80
AJ Stewart (ENG)	1990–2003	33	44	78
ATW Grout (AUS)	1958–1966	22	41	76
TG Evans (ENG)	1946–1959	31	59	76
MJ Prior (ENG)	2009–2013	18	34	63
JJ Kelly (AUS)	1896–1905	33	61	55
H Carter (AUS)	1907–1921	21	41	52

MOST ASHES CATCHES

PLAYER	CAREER	MAT	INNS	CT
IT Botham (ENG)	1977–1989	32	62	54
AR Border (AUS)	1978–1993	42	79	51
GS Chappell (AUS)	1970–1983	30	58	48
MA Taylor (AUS)	1989–1999	33	65	46
H Trumble (AUS)	1890–1904	31	59	45
ME Waugh (AUS)	1991–2001	29	58	43
WR Hammond (ENG)	1928–1947	33	59	43
RT Ponting (AUS)	1997–2010	35	67	41
MC Cowdrey (ENG)	1954–1975	43	80	40
LC Braund (ENG)	1901–1908	20	38	37
AN Cook (ENG)	2006–2015	30	56	37
WW Armstrong (AUS)	1902–1921	42	80	37

MOST ASHES WICKETS

PLAYER	CAREER	MAT	INNS	WKTS	BBM
SK Warne (AUS)	1993–2007	36	72	195	8/71
GD McGrath (AUS)	1994–2007	30	60	157	8/38
H Trumble (AUS)	1890–1904	31	55	141	8/65
DK Lillee (AUS)	1971–1982	24	47	128	7/89
IT Botham (ENG)	1977–1989	32	58	128	6/95
RGD Willis (ENG)	1971–1983	31	61	123	8/43
MA Noble (AUS)	1898–1909	39	66	115	7/17
RR Lindwall (AUS)	1946–1959	29	51	114	7/63
W Rhodes (ENG)	1899–1926	41	65	109	8/6
SF Barnes (ENG)	1901–1912	20	36	106	7/60
CV Grimmett (AUS)	1925–1934	22	39	106	6/37
AV Bedser (ENG)	1946–1954	21	37	104	7/44
WJ O'Reilly (AUS)	1932–1938	19	33	102	7/54
CTB Turner (AUS)	1887–1895	17	30	101	7/43
R Peel (ENG)	1884–1896	20	35	101	7/31
G Giffen (AUS)	1882–1896	26	40	101	7/117
TM Alderman (AUS)	1981–1991	17	32	100	6/47

BIBLIOGRAPHY

Arnold, P and P Wynne-Thomas *The Ashes: A Complete Illustrated History*, Axiom, Adelaide, 1990.

Cashman, R *The Oxford Companion of Australian Cricket*, Oxford University Press, Melbourne, 1996.

Davis, C *Test Cricket in Australia 1877–2002*, self-published, Victoria, 2002.

Dawson, M *Memorable Ashes Moments, 1861–2007* ABC Books, Sydney, 2009.

Foster, D and P Arnold *100 Years of Test Cricket, England v Australia*, Hamlyn Publishing Group, 1977.

Frindall, B *The Wisden Book of Test Cricket, Volumes 1 and 2*, Headline Book Publishing, Surrey, 1995.

Frith, D *England Versus Australia: A Pictorial History of Test Matches* since 1877, Rigby, Adelaide, 1977.

Hill, L R *Australian Cricketers on Tour 1968–1974*, Lynton Publications, Blackwood, 1974.

Martin Jenkins, C *The Complete Who's Who of Test Cricketers*, Rigby, Australia, 1983.

Nicholls, B *The Establishment Boys*, New Holland Publishers, 2015

Nicholls, B *Test of the Century*, New Holland Publishers, 2016

Osmond, R *The Battle for the Ashes,* Worth Press Limited, 2006.

Webster, R *First-class Cricket in Australia Vols 1 and 2*, self-published, Melbourne, 1997.

Whimpress, B *The Official Ashes Treasures,* Allen & Unwin, Australia, 2013.

Websites

espncricinfo.com

Howstat.com

www.bbc.com

www.abc.net.au/news/sport

UK £14.99